SpringerBriefs in Psychology

SpringerBriefs present concise summaries of cutting-edge research and practical applications across a wide spectrum of fields. Featuring compact volumes of 50 to 125 pages, the series covers a range of content from professional to academic. Typical topics might include:

- A timely report of state-of-the-art analytical techniques
- A bridge between new research results as published in journal articles and a contextual literature review
- A snapshot of a hot or emerging topic
- An in-depth case study or clinical example
- A presentation of core concepts that readers must understand to make independent contributions

SpringerBriefs in Psychology showcase emerging theory, empirical research, and practical application in a wide variety of topics in psychology and related fields. Briefs are characterized by fast, global electronic dissemination, standard publishing contracts, standardized manuscript preparation and formatting guidelines, and expedited production schedules.

More information about this series at http://www.springer.com/series/10143

Robert Henley Woody

Risks of Harm from Psychopathic Individuals

Springer

Robert Henley Woody
Department of Psychology
University of Nebraska at Omaha
Omaha, NE, USA

ISSN 2192-8363 ISSN 2192-8371 (electronic)
SpringerBriefs in Psychology
ISBN 978-3-030-20997-1 ISBN 978-3-030-20998-8 (eBook)
https://doi.org/10.1007/978-3-030-20998-8

This Springer imprint is published by the registered company Springer Nature Switzerland AG
The registered company address is: Gewerbestrasse 11, 6330 Cham, Switzerland

This book is dedicated to the personnel associated with the Florida Department of Law Enforcement and anyone who needs help dealing with the increasing amount of psychopathy that plagues modern society.

Preface

With a somewhat busy street just to her left and greenery to her right, she did her morning jog in the city park, enjoying the music that was playing in her earphones. That was the last thing that she remembered until she awakened in the hospital.

She was a highly trained law professional and demonstrated her confidence in a courtroom routinely. Jogging early in the morning in that particular location did not raise any safety concerns. However, her confidence was inadequate protection against the male who jumped out of the bushes that she had just passed, hit her on the head with some object, started sexually assaulting her but stopped when he apparently became fearful of detection by a passing motorist. Before passing out, she realized that he was unknown to her.

The attacker pushed her unconscious body into the adjacent shallow stream. Thankfully her face was up, which allowed her to breathe. She healed physically, but the traumatic effects continue for her and her family.

Too often, most people think things like: "This is a safe area." "I can defend myself." "If I were attacked, someone would stop their car and come to my aid." "It can't happen to me." In this day and age, all of those notions of personal security are potentially false.

When I was a teenager, several youths started yelling obscenities from across the street, basically voicing threats. The fellow with whom I was walking (to a concert in a downtown area) said foolishly "I don't believe in fisticuffs or weapons. If those guys tried to start a fight, I bet I could talk them out of it."

No matter where it might be, constant vigilance and competency for self-protection are essential when one is "out and about." For example, many people believe that a university campus is commonly a safe location, but contemporary societal conditions justify a full-service law enforcement agency on every campus.

The information that I provide herein is intended for everyone. In this day and age, regrettably we all encounter the effects of the psychopathology possessed by other people. Therefore, where there is a friend, co-worker/employee, acquaintance, or family member with psychopathic characteristics, the information here will be helpful for managing the communications and contacts with them. For professionals in the human services (e.g., mental health practitioners, healthcare providers, and educators), this information will build knowledge and skills that can be extended to clients, patients, and others.

Omaha, USA Robert Henley Woody

Critical Terms

The following terms provide (in a purposeful lexical sequence) the foundation for the contents and are quoted from: VandenBos, G. R. (2015). *APA dictionary of psychology* (2nd ed.). Washington, DC: American Psychological Association. The selection is intended to further the concept of maintaining safety for self, others, rights, or objects.

AVOIDANCE: "The practice or an instance of keeping away from particular situations, individuals, or things because of either (a) the anticipated negative or consequence of such an encounter or (b) anxious or painful feelings associated with them." (p. 100–101).
AVOIDANCE BEHAVIOR: "any act or series of actions that enables an individual to avoid or anticipate unpleasant or painful situations, stimuli, or events including conditioned aversive stimuli." (p. 101)
VICTIM: "an individual who is the target of another person's violent, discriminatory, harassing, or assaultive behaviors." (p. 1138)
ASSAULT: "a violent attack on an individual" and "illegal conduct occurring when an individual either attempts to injure another person or threatens to do so and has capacity to carry out the threat." (p. 80)
HARM REDUCTION: "an approach designed to reduce the adverse effects of risky behaviors (e.g., alcohol use, drug use, indiscriminate sexual activity), rather than to eliminate the behaviors altogether." (p. 483)
SAFETY PSYCHOLOGY: "a subdiscipline of applied psychology involving the study of behavioral aspects of hazardous situations in human-environmental systems . . . ." (p. 931)
TRUST: "reliance on or confidence in the dependability of someone or something. In interpersonal relationships, trust refers to the confidence that a person or group of people has in the reliability of another person or group . . . . The key factor is not the intrinsic honesty of the other people but their predictability." (p. 1110)
VIGILANCE: "A state of extreme awareness and watchfulness directed by one or more members of a group toward the environment, often toward potential threats (e.g., predators, intruders, enemy forces in combat)." (p. 1119)

Contents

About the Author

Robert Henley Woody is Professor of Psychology (and former Dean for Graduate Studies and Research) at the University of Nebraska Omaha (1975–Present) and an attorney in private practice (1981–Present). Before coming to the University of Nebraska Omaha, he held professorships at the State University of New York at Buffalo, the University of Maryland, the Ohio University, and the Grand Valley State University. Previously, he was a public school teacher, school psychologist, and director of special education.

He received a Doctor of Philosophy degree from the Michigan State University, a Doctor of Science degree from the University of Pittsburgh Graduate School of Public Health, and a Juris Doctor degree from the Creighton University School of Law. He was a postdoctoral fellow in clinical psychology at the University of London Institute of Psychiatry and earned the two-year Certificate in Group Psychotherapy from the Washington School of Psychiatry. Also, he graduated from the Basic Police Academy at the Pat Thomas Law Enforcement Academy (Tallahassee).

He is a licensed psychologist in Michigan, and admitted to the Florida, Michigan, and Nebraska Bars. The American Board of Professional Psychology has named him a Diplomate in Clinical Psychology and a Diplomate in Forensic Psychology, and the American Board of Assessment Psychology has deemed him to be a Diplomate in Assessment Psychology. The American Psychological Association (APA) and the American Association for Marriage and Family Therapy (AAMFT) have accorded him the status of Fellow, and with the American Association of Sexuality Educators, Counselors and Therapists (AASECT), he is a certified sex therapist emeritus.

Chapter 1
Accentuating the Positive

Although mental illness does not always create a danger of violence, the decrease in social agencies, mental health services, and other support and treatment sources in the community have led to an increase in risks. Moreover, locations differ greatly in the availability of resources. The need, however, is everywhere. Estimates vary, but it has been asserted that at any one time 20% of the population could benefit from professional mental health services. This may be an understatement.

Since risks and crimes decrease the quality of life in contemporary society, everyone is impacted by crime. Research reports vary but seem to indicate that about one in five people might be characterized as psychopathic, that is, have antisocial personality disorders. These are people who are likely to inflict negative and harmful conditions, including violence, on others and have no remorse.

When I was in the police academy, each day ended with an instructor warning the trainees: "Be careful, there are people out there who will kill you and go home and sleep like a baby." We were instructed to not wear any signs of involvement with law enforcement unless we had our weaponry as well. The bottom line is, as readers will recognize from news reports and "cop shows" on contemporary television, the risk of harm is everywhere and constant.

Psychopathy seems to be increasing. I will tell you about the characteristics of those in everyday life who may merit this label; and based on behavioral science research, I will provide information about the likely causes of psychopathy. I will describe scholarly information that indicates a strong connection between crime and psychopathy. Regrettably those people with psychopathy are apt to continue the criminal pattern throughout life. I will explain psychopathy in detail and offer suggestions for safety and managing the effects of psychopathy in others.

Crime can involve, of course, property or legal rights. My emphasis will be, however, on the individual's personal mental and physical well-being and maximizing one's safety to protect against harm, including preventive measures that everyone needs to maintain.

R. H. Woody, *Risks of Harm from Psychopathic Individuals*, SpringerBriefs in Psychology, https://doi.org/10.1007/978-3-030-20998-8_1

A long-standing view is that psychopathic criminals "wear a mask of sanity." My assertion is that they are "Great Pretenders," who are a high risk of committing crimes. Despite appearing to be "normal" and "peaceful" at times, they pose danger to others, such as with domestic violence, stressful marriage and other relationships, harassment of others, etc. However, it is worth remembering that not all people with psychopathy are violent and not all people who commit violence have psychopathy.

Every person with any degree of logic and sensibility wants to avoid painful or detrimental encounters. The reality of life requires acceptance of the fact that no one can be assuredly free from negative conditions. That said, a person can and should exercise caution to maximize safety and health, with the goal of preventing discomfort, physical and mental illnesses, accidental injuries, victimization by crimes, and death.

Regrettably, the conditions in everyday life offer no guarantee that the most prudent decisions and life style assure positive outcomes. To quote the old saw, the only thing assured are death and taxes. One of my friends often quips, "We all have to die sometime." Said bluntly, during one's life span, misfortune will enter into everyone's life. The platform for life should be: I shall take responsibility for avoiding the negative and accentuating the positive (an old song): "You've got to accentuate the positive, Eliminate the negative, Latch on to the affirmative, But don't mess with mister in between" (Mercer and Arlen 1945).

My message here is not to predict bad things to come. The purpose is to offer understanding and insight into how to define, establish, and maintain personal safety and gratification that can minimize the risks of negative experiences.

As a student of history, I have found the amount of violence that humans have imposed on others to be downright shocking. Often the tactics have been bizarre, the common dimension has been the blatant disregard of civility. As I mentioned earlier, the police academy instructors' warning against "people who will kill you and go home and sleep like a baby" was not said in jest. In reality there are people who do not value the life or rights of others. This lack of social responsibility is suggestive of psychopathic others.

In this day and age, especially when someone resorts to profound violence, such as a shooting spree, the public is often prone to allege that the perpetrator had been deprived of good parenting. The notion is that parents or caregivers could and should be able to stem or prevent violence in the youngsters. In theory, such a viewpoint cannot be disputed; however, some children with caring parents misbehave and can get reinforced by various conditions. Certainly bullying may, in fact, be reinforced by ineffective parenting, perhaps exacerbated by a neurological response, which contradicts abstaining from violence.

Siblings or "buddies," male or female, regardless of age, may reinforce inappropriate conduct by others. Here is where effective parenting comes into play. The old saying, "You are known by the company that you keep," means that parents need to be aware of who might be reinforcing a child's aggressive behavior.

Moreover, the interactions (e.g., between relatives, parents and caregivers with a youth) are critical. Some of these influences may be by chance alone.

Although my father died of a stroke when I was thirteen and I was an only child, my maternal grandmother was my primary caregiver, helping my working mother. In retrospect, both of them were quite dutiful in guiding me to avoid foolishness and dangers. For everyone, those are priceless qualities, and I was fortunate.

With this guidance, I developed a distinct aversion to harm, whether to self or others. My adult knowledge and training in health, law, and psychology subsequently strengthened my social values and law-abiding conduct. Nowadays, I seldom watch television or go to movies because of the scripts' penchant for violence.

Watching violence on television can lead to unfortunate observational learning. Huesmann et al. say (2003): "Overall, these results suggest that both males and females from all social strata and all levels of initial aggressiveness are placed at increased risk for the development of adult aggressive and violent behavior when they view a high and steady diet of violent TV shows in early childhood" (p. 218). From their analysis of the effects of violent media, Bartol and Bartol (2019) conclude: "The researchers suggest that the easiest way to reduce the effects of media violence on children is to restrict children's exposure to such violence" (p. 290), and they call for parents or caretakers to be responsible. Said bluntly, for values relevant to constructive ideas and conduct, there is logical support for caution about and avoidance of the violence portrayed in modern-day mass media.

In sum, yes, human beings have a fascination for violence, and death and destruction depicted in the so-called "entertainment" media, and these do not "cause" psychopathy. But individuals vary as to what they find reinforcing. And despite parental oversight, chance occurrences and individual differences can reinforce anti-social behavior.

References

Bartol, C. R., & Bartol, A. M. (2019). *Introduction to forensic psychology* (5th ed.). Thousand Oaks, CA: Sage.

Huesmann, L. R., Moise-Titus, J., Podolski, C. L., & Eron, L. D. (2003). Longitudinal relations between children's exposure to TV violence and their aggressiveness and violent behavior in young adulthood: 1977–1992. *Developmental Psychology, 39,* 201–221.

Mercer, J., & Arlen, H. (1945). *Accentuate the positive*. Publisher Edwin H. Morris & Co.

Chapter 2
Harm in Contemporary Society

Contemporary societal conditions wield the proverbial "double-edged sword." In the book, *A Tale of Two Cities*, Charles Dickens is credited with: "It was the best of times, it was the worst of times, it was the age of wisdom, it was the age of foolishness, it was the epoch of belief, it was the epoch of incredulity, it was the season of Light, it was the season of Darkness …." (https://www.shmoop.com/quotes/best-of-times-worst-of-times.htm).

As compared to yesteryear, contemporary society is remarkably blessed. Many commonplace hardships have been eliminated. Nonetheless, we cannot live our current daily lives without risks of harm.

Whether alone or in groups, the human condition creates mental and physical vulnerability. Mental injury comes from sensing insults from others, our own negative self-attributions, not to mention overt condemnation and avoidance from others. Physical vulnerability results when circumstances allow for purposeful attacks by one or more others.

The social and behavioral sciences leave no doubt that human beings (and animals) in general are prone to harm others. Psychopaths feel entitled to take resources, regardless of ownership and without compensation. For example, they may steal minor or valuable property or assets and have no regret or remorse.

In every society (i.e., an interactive group of humans), individual needs, from defenses for survival to emotional exchanges, are commonly dependent on others for fulfillment. Of course, when someone else is involved, it is likely and logical that he or she will expect a *quid pro quo*. There is an expectation of reciprocity of benefits, that is, payment or compensation. In legal parlance, it is a matter of "consideration." The old adage, "You get what you pay for" is applicable.

Recognizing vulnerability to both physical and mental harm, people must be wary. There should be no unjustified trust; there should be a prudent judgment as to whether certain people or situations are dangerous or create a risk to one's person, property, or rights. Risks must be identified and protection must be implemented.

R. H. Woody, *Risks of Harm from Psychopathic Individuals*, SpringerBriefs in Psychology, https://doi.org/10.1007/978-3-030-20998-8_2

It can go without saying perhaps that people vary in their definition of risks, and some folks are more vulnerable than others to a risk imposing harm. For example, I am often amazed that people will walk a dangerous trail, figuratively or literally, or enter into a situation that to me, with what might be my hyper-prudence, should be avoided.

This insight comes from awareness of, at my stage of life. That is, my survival qualities (e.g., balance, strength, etc.) are not now what they once were in my younger years: Yes, I ran for years, including marathons. Yes, in the police academy, I enjoyed greatly the rough-and-tumble defensive tactics (including with my 313-pound training partner, when I weighed much less). Yes, I hiked almost every rugged trail in the Rocky Mountain National Park. Today as a "senior" by any definition, I realize that it would be foolish for me to undertake the risks that are associated with such endeavors.

Psychological research has revealed that the power of certain psychological needs varies at different life stages. The attributions assigned to a given age of the person are often more stereotypes than reality. For example, in my mid-60s I graduated from a full-fledged law enforcement academy (yes, it was challenging physically).

Said bluntly, categorizing a person for needs or risks is, more often than not, spurious. As an example, consider crowding: "psychological tension produced in environments of high population density, especially when individuals feel that the amount of space available to them is insufficient for their needs" (VandenBos 2015, p. 270). One often hears that research supports that: people in crowding conditions are prone to experience anxiety, perhaps even leading to mental and physical deterioration; societal aggression or workplace violence may be most characteristic of the teenage and young or mid-adult years; and those same younger years may heighten a need for excitement and a sense of invincibility. In other words, there are some social contexts for some people, but not all, that will accommodate violence.

Of course, some characteristics, such as engaging in terrorism, abuse of others, and being shaped by the mass media (be it positively or negatively) defy pigeonholing just by age alone. All of the foregoing characteristics have exceptions. Comments about age-related qualities (or lack thereof) are often spurious and stereotypical at best.

With the presence of psychopaths in society, it seems that a justifiable summation would be trust no one! There is no doubt that certain conditions, such as survival and narcissistic motivation of extreme self-enhancement, can lead to harm for others. The first step towards social responsibility is a commitment to respect, honor, and safeguard—whether it involves people, animals, property, or rights.

To get the message across, when I teach a university course on forensic psychology, I make a point to ask the students a hypothetical: "What would you do if your son or daughter were kidnapped; you knew who did the crime, but your local law enforcement would not act effectively?" Commonly, the inappropriate choice of "self help" (i.e., "taking the law into one's own hands") surfaces, notwithstanding the influence coming from a fictitious Clint Eastwood movie.

Due to human nature, narcissistic motivation is all too common in essentially any interaction or relationship, and creates an omnipresent risk of potential harm for friendships and family relations. Family abuse may take the form of neglect, emotional and physical harm, and countless other ways that one family member or person member may be intentionally or unintentionally hurtful toward another family member or person (note the next chapter deals with risk taking). For example, even an accident may have a connection to carelessness. Hurting a friend or family member reveals the extent of application of my earlier comments about trust no one!"

Reference

VandenBos, G. R. (2015). *APA dictionary of psychology* (2nd ed.). Washington, DC: American Psychological Association.

Chapter 3
Risk Taking

About a half century-plus ago, only about 15% of automobile accidents occurred by pure chance (Coleman 1956). Some drivers are more accident prone than others. Again, early on, approximately 75% of all automobile accidents were caused by about ten percent of the population (Bristol 1936). Although questionable for exactness, those types of numbers are now ill defined, but it seems probable that the risk from driving has increased (i.e., due to increased numbers of car, speed, distractions, etc.).

The idea of an "accident prone personality" is nothing new. In his 1901 classic *Psychopathology of Everyday Life*, Sigmund Freud said (as translated by A. A. Brill):

> many apparently accidental injuries happening … are really self-inflicted. This is brought about by the fact that there is a constantly lurking tendency to self-punishment, usually expressing itself in self-reproach, or contributing to the formulation of a symptom, which skillfully makes use of an external situation. The required external situations may accidentally present itself or the punishment tendency may assist it until the way is open for the desired injurious effect (Freud 1951, p. 96).

In other words, the underlying premise is that accidents are caused by an individual's psychological characteristics.

Greek mythology personified death with the name thanatos, the brother of sleep. Psychoanalytic theory adopted the term "thanatos" for a theoretical set of strivings devoted to reduction of tension in life activities. Psychoanalytic theory linked the motives to eros (love) and sexual strivings and other constructs in life. The idea was that everyone has the potential to succumb to a thanatos-based motive (i.e., accepting death as a solution).

Indeed, it may seem that there are some people who, as compared to others, are prone to accidents or experiencing bad luck. Emerging in the early 20th century out of psychoanalytic theory and thanatos, the concept of "accident proneness" has long been debated. That is, only some sources believe that there is such a thing as a fixed accident-prone personality composite.

Another motivational thrust in psychoanalytic theory comes from suicide ideation, as well as thoughts and preoccupation with self-harm that can lead to death. Suicidal

R. H. Woody, *Risks of Harm from Psychopathic Individuals*, SpringerBriefs in Psychology, https://doi.org/10.1007/978-3-030-20998-8_3

ideation or obsessions often occur in a context of a major depressive episode, which can be promoted by, say, substance abuse. There may or may not be a concomitant of a psychiatric disorder, extreme grief from trauma, or untenable contextual situations (e.g., divorce, loss of employment, etc.). Due to social modeling (i.e., being influenced by what is reinforced) or genetics, there is risk created for some offspring when, say, a parent, such as those who are accident prone, careless, or suicidal.

From genetics, analysis of the psychological fundamentals of safety starts with the idea of possible historical determinism, that is, the power of one's history can trigger a concept of psychopathology. This notion is the prelude to accident proneness. As will be quickly evident, a historical launching pad will be used to move to a modern trajectory.

At the threshold of the concept of accident proneness are several basic questions. Why do some people seem to be involved in more accidents than others? Is it a matter of happenstance, bad luck, moral retribution, or personal psychological characteristics? According to VandenBos (2015), accident proneness is described as: "a chronic susceptibility to accidents" (p. 8). This concept has been heavily debated since it was introduced around 1920, and many scholarly theoreticians question the existence of a fixed accident-prone personality. However, a variety of individual variables and sociological and environmental (situational) factors have been identified as important predictors of accident involvement. These include "aggressiveness, impulsiveness, thrill and adventure seeking, workload and cognitive demand, and stress" (p. 8).

Although not said in the foregoing source (but connected to aggressiveness), it seems that inherent hostility towards self or others may well be a harbinger for the characteristics relevant to accident proneness. As is logical, the hostile person may also be narcissistic and likely to channel that characteristic into exposure to risks and harmful ventures towards self or others.

In accord with these early ideas from Freud, a significant number of persons involved in automobile accidents seem to have certain unique psychological characteristics (James and Dickinson 1950; Woody 1980). Research finds minimal causation from habits and skills (e.g., poor driving habits), physical characteristics (e.g., visual acuity), and psychomotor characteristics (e.g., stimulus-response measures, coordination).

Although it is commonly thought that persons under 25 and over 65 have historically experienced a disproportionately large share of automobile accidents, it seems doubtful that age, years of driving, or other experiences are distinctive. However, there is reason to believe that emotional disturbance may correlate positively with accident proneness when driving and engaging in other activities.

Being prone to have automobile accidents seems in general to be linked to neurotic personality traits, egocentricity, resentment of authority, exhibitionism, impulsivity, a lack of social responsibility, aggressiveness, anger (especially towards sources of authority), guilt, inadequate regard for pain (and perhaps even pleasure from pain or the thrill and excitement of being hurt), depression, restlessness, and certain phobias (e.g., agoraphobia, claustrophobia, and fear of falling) (James and Dickinson 1950).

It may be that unstable persons, such as those who are prone to being stressed easily, react concurrently to both the traffic and his or her own fantasies of violence, aggression, fear, and power as symbolized by the traffic. In other words, the likelihood of an unstable person's doing something foolish or am inappropriate thing is increased. James and Dickinson issue a wise caveat: "accident proneness means a predisposition to have an undue number of accidents, but the high-accident group may contain some individuals who are not accident-prone" (p. 771). Also, it is logical that the array of psychological characteristics cited do not necessarily assure that persons with those descriptors will, in fact, have an elevated risk of accident proneness.

From the aforesaid psychodynamic ideas, it would hold that many accidents are due to a failure of the ego function of self preservation, with childhood being the proving ground: "A neglected child has no model to follow [to be safe] and an overindulged and overprotected child may not assume responsibility for himself. Expressing oneself in deeds, rather than in fantasies, thoughts, or words, is a major cause of accident proneness" (Kessler 1966, p. 349). She goes on to say that flawed development of the superego leads the child to turn aggression inward and to have an unconscious acknowledgement of both anger and its objects, with the self-provoked injury serving to relieve feelings of guilt. Incidentally, Greenson (1967) postulates that accident proneness may be manifested in a framework of transference-related hostility involving a therapist.

In what some mental health scholars might consider to be the ultimate treatise on psychoanalytic ideas, Fenichel (1945) describes how a person may recognize a lack of omnipotence but seeks adult omnipotence and power to shape ego ideals, gathering reassurances from many sources to salve guilt feelings: "the more power a person has, the less he needs to justify his acts. An increase in self esteem means a decrease in guilt feelings" (p. 500). This may lead to risky behavior, such as crimes, to assuage guilt feelings: "These crimes may then be committed in an attempt to prove to oneself that one may commit them without being punished, that is, in an attempt to repress guilt feelings" (p. 500).

With the guilt being the fuel for ego and superego clashes, the possibility of accident proneness enters the picture. Fenichel states: "Instead of powerful rebellion one may seek ingratiation through sacrifices, thorough suffering, and through becoming the victim of unconsciously arranged accidents .... There are also persons who experience accident after accident without ever being able to lacerate their strict superego, or who arrange their lives so that they suffer one reverse after another in miserable 'neuroses of destiny'" (pp. 500–501; other citations omitted).

When an adverse or negative condition, such as an accident, arises in one's life, the anxiety may be witnessed in a propensity for physical problems, such as a conversion neurosis: "Frequently, the conversion symptoms are sufficiently prominent so that compensation neuroses are often classified among the hysterias" (Kolb 1977, p. 521). When an accident neurosis occurs, "the symptoms include irritability, stubbornness, argumentativeness, crying spells, anxiety, depression, sleeplessness, headache, and dizziness," along with possible "complaints of poor memory and inability to concentrate" (p. 522). Certainly these kinds of symptoms elevate the risk for a lapse in psychological safety that relies on emotional, cognitive, and behavioral processes.

To summarize, psychoanalytic concepts of an accident prone personality hold that there is an unconscious attempt to negate longstanding instinctual conflicts and to find either belated gratification for repressed impulses or relief from inner tension. In any case, the person is presumed to be a victim of his or her psychological makeup.

In modern mental health research, psychoanalytic concepts are often subject to disparagement. Regardless, psychoanalytic principles and speculations have withstood the onslaught of behaviorism and other personality and intervention theories, those that advocated consciousness rather than unconsciousness, and those that relied upon reinforcement theory. As Benjamin (2014) says pointedly:

> Go into any bookstore and look at the titles that are on the shelves labeled "Psychology." Count the number of full-length biographies published on Freud (perhaps nearly 70, although all are not currently in print). Count the number on Wundt–there is one. When it comes to public access of psychology, psychoanalysis is still the stuff of talk shows, movies, magazine articles, and self-help programs (p. 138).

Of course psychoanalytic ideas are not the only sources for understanding risk taking, but they still merit consideration.

References

Benjamin, L. T., Jr. (2014). *A brief history of modern psychology* (2nd ed.). Hoboken, NJ: Wiley.

Bristol. (1936). Medical aspects of accident control. 107 *JAMA* 653.

Coleman, J. C. (1956). *Abnormal psychology and modern life* (2nd ed.). Chicago: Scott, Foresman.

Fenichel, O. (1945). *The psychoanalytic theory of neurosis*. New York: Norton.

Freud, S. (1951). *Psychopathology of everyday life*. New York: Mentor (New American Library).

Greenson, R. R. (1967). *The technique and practice of psychoanalysis* (Vol. 1). New York: International Universities Press.

James, F., Jr., & Dickenson, J. J. (1950). Accident proneness and accident law. *Harvard Law Review, 63*, 769–795.

Kessler, J. (1966). *Psychopathology of childhood*. Englewood Cliffs, NJ: Prentice-Hall.

Kolb, L. C. (1977). *Modern clinical psychiatry*. Philadelphia: W. B. Saunders.

VandenBos, G. R. (2015). *APA dictionary of psychology* (2nd ed.). Washington, DC: American Psychological Association.

Woody, R. H. (1980). Accident proneness. *Medical Trial Technique Quarterly, 27*(1), 74–82.

Chapter 4
Deception: The Great Pretender

It is human nature to want others to share and endorse our preferences. The other person, however, may resist any overture to take away his or her independence in self-related determinations. To counteract and persuade, deception may be used to try to create acceptance of personal values by other people.

Efforts to influence another person can create a risk of rejection, retaliation, or avoidance. There is the possibility of so-called psychological reactance. VandenBos (2015) tells us that reactance theory is "a model stating that in response to a perceived threat to—or loss of—a behavioral freedom, a person will experience psychological reactance (or more simply, reactance), a motivational state characterized by distress, anxiety, resistance, and the desire to restore that freedom" (p. 883).

Some folks (myself included) respond with strong opposition to another person's attempt to control. Consciously or unconsciously, they believe that personal independence is being denied or threatened. VandenBos continues, "According to this model, when people feel coerced into a certain behavior, they will react against the coercion, often by demonstrating an increased preference for the behavior that is restrained, and may perform the behavior opposite of what is desired" (p. 883).

Beyond the need to influence or control others, some individuals seem predisposed to self-enhancement through deception. In the 1955 song, *The Great Pretender* (Peer Music) was popularized by the music group, the Platters (and in 1987, the sometimes outrageous Freddy Mercury). The lyrics assert that being a "great pretender, pretending that I'm doing well" is followed by a confession that "I'm lonely but no one can tell." The punch line is "I seem to be what I'm not, you see." As the lyrical story progresses, a departed love interest is lamented, and there is an admission of "Just laughin' and gay like a clown … pretending that you're still around." Whether or not the composer, Buck Ram, knew it at the time, the lyrics capture a signature characteristic of psychopathy (nowadays considered to be an antisocial personality disorder [ASD]).

R. H. Woody, *Risks of Harm from Psychopathic Individuals*, SpringerBriefs in Psychology, https://doi.org/10.1007/978-3-030-20998-8_4

The underlying causation for both attempts at controlling and deceiving another person are products of a mental disorder stemming from insecurity and loneliness, which lead to depression and deceitful behavior. The outcome is fueled by narcissism, a false ordainment of superiority, which continues–commonly throughout the life of the "pretender" and imposes extreme hurt on self and others. The narcissistic personality contains "a pattern of traits and behaviors characterized by excessive self-concern and overvaluation of the self" (VandenBos 2015, p. 686).

Many interpersonal relationships are complicated by the presence of a personality disorder for one or more participants. With personality disorders, there are three clusters: "Cluster A includes paranoid, schizoid, and schizotypal; Cluster B includes antisocial, borderline, histrionic, and narcissistic; and Cluster C includes avoidance, dependent, and obsessive-compulsive" (VandenBos 2015, p. 783). Whether an encounter in everyday life or in the context of professional service, it is difficult to escape the snare of character or personality disorders in people with whom there is interaction.

Over the years, as I will discuss, there has been a string of descriptors for the clusters of characteristics associated with psychopathy. As noted already, recently the term antisocial personality disorder (ASD) seems to be the preferred term for the many descriptors of psychopathic personality characteristics. I tend to use the two terms interchangeably. For the purpose herein, each of the terms mentioned seems appropriate for consideration, albeit that some reflect more the historical point in time, as opposed to the here and now.

The contemporary scholarship on psychopathy distinguishes ASD from other relevant and often overlapping definitions and terminologies. Etiology is considered (i.e., whether the roots spring from neurological conditions, culture, social learning, or a combination), and it is noted that the propensity for deception and manipulation is present with both psychopathic characteristics in general and is a manifestation of ASD in specific. Regardless of the terminology, there is disregard for and violation of the rights of others. Aristotle called attention to "evil intent" (Miller 2012), which was, for the time, a warning about psychopathic characteristics.

Caution: The distinction between ASD and psychopathy is sometimes vague and misleading. Many individuals with psychopathic characteristics wear a disguise of a "mask of sanity" (as described in the aforementioned song lyrics), a term popularized by Cleckley (1941).

Notwithstanding or because of their seemingly positive characteristics (which may come and go), psychopaths tend to violate the rights of others without being subjected to the criminal justice system. They may evade detection because of consciously or unconsciously feigned sociability (e.g., seeming to be charming or uniquely competent). Despite their positive accomplishments, as well as denials and protestations, psychopaths have the potential for harmful and violent acts.

Ironically, as I was writing the Preface for this book, a friend asked, "Can a psychopath be just a little bit psychopathic?" What was being asked, of course, was whether there are degrees of psychopathy? The answer is yes, indeed. A Great Pretender may have many strengths and good qualities, but it is important to be wary of deception.

As Hare (1999) puts it: "be aware that people who are not psychopaths may have some of the symptoms .... Psychopathy is a syndrome—a cluster of related symptoms" (p. 34). However, the positive characteristics that are evidenced may be transitory or contradicted by pathology. Positive actions may mask, but do not erase psychopathy.

ASD often begins in childhood or early adolescence and continues on into adulthood. I will review research on the incidence of psychopathy (and the associated problems in obtaining a realistic estimate), criminal psychopaths, and violent psychopathy. It seems that permissive societal conditions reinforce narcissism and irresponsibility (e.g., which may also receive reinforcement by the mass media). Further, attitudes about mental health and the demise of community mental health services seem to allow psychopathy to go undetected and consequently increase abuse of and threats to others.

Later I will consider ways to manage people with ASD. Regrettably, the notion of a "cure" cannot be fulfilled; that is, as will be explained authoritatively, the best that can be accomplished with psychopaths is modification and control. The Great Pretender is, unfortunately, under the enduring control of psychopathy. DeLisi (2016) considers psychopathic characteristics to be a "life course."

To be clear, the framework for the information that I will present is not limited to antisocial personality disorder (ASD), psychopathy, or sociopathy. The spotlight is on deception or pretending in order to engage in unhealthy and potentially harmful ways with other people. The primary message is: Being warned about the psychological characteristics (i.e., emotions, cognitions, and conduct) that feed into deception can prepare the reader to avoid victimization by a Great Pretender.

References

Cleckley, H. (1941). *The mask of sanity*. St. Louis, MO: C. V. Mosby.

DeLisi, M. (2016). *Psychopathy as unified theory of crime*. New York: Palgrave Macmillan.

Hare, R. D. (1999). *Without conscience: The disturbing world of the psychopaths among us*. New York: Guilford.

Miller, L. (2012). *Criminal psychology: Nature, nurture, culture*. Springfield, IL: Charles C Thomas.

VandenBos, G. R. (2015). *APA dictionary of psychology* (2nd ed.). Washington, DC: American Psychological Association.

Chapter 5
The Term Psychopathy

The term "psychopath" commonly triggers concern and fear: "Indeed when presented with the term psychopath, laypersons who are asked to think of associated descriptors often respond with words such as evil and monster" (Douglas et al. 2015, p. 257). Previously, I mentioned Aristotle's centuries-old pejorative of "evil intent."

Stigmatizing mental illness is "fostered and strengthened by television shows movies and news outlets that regularly portray people with often-unnamed mental illnesses as being dangerous or incompetent" (Franzoi 2016, p. 239). Although psychopathy "elevates the risk of crime and violence" (Douglas et al. 2015, p. 306), a criminal propensity may or may not be present with a given psychopath. That said, psychopaths are, indeed, dangerous in many ways, but not necessarily in a criminal or physically violent manner.

An apt reminder of the preceding principle is the book title, *The Sociopath Next Door* (Stout 2005). Her view is that a psychopath or sociopath is likely within every person's life space and can inflict great injury to persons, property, rights, or society without resorting to physical violence per se. This viewpoint supports my assertion of trust no one.

If a person possesses certain characteristics associated with the term "psychopath," as defined herein, then he or she possesses the potential to, at some point and under certain conditions, act in a destructive manner. Consequently, the term "sociopathy" nowadays refers to a "psychopath" who has, in fact, acted in a criminal way (with or without prosecution by the legal system). The belief that a sociopath, unlike the psychopath, is aware of hurting others (i.e., potentially has empathy) remains for conjecture. Douglas et al. (2015) analyze and discuss numerous debated theories and issues pertaining to psychopathy.

The one undeniable descriptor for people within the realm of psychopathy and sociopathy categories is "abusive." In his book "*The Abusive Personality*," Dutton (2003) states emphatically: "A triad of early factors—witnessing abuse, being shamed by a parent, and being insecurely attached through unpredictable parental emotional

R. H. Woody, *Risks of Harm from Psychopathic Individuals*, SpringerBriefs in Psychology, https://doi.org/10.1007/978-3-030-20998-8_5

availability—constitute the basis of the adult abusive personality" (p. viii). As I will present, clinical experience and research reveal that the psychopath has more complex etiology than Dutton's triad, although those three childhood conditions are almost always present—but there may be genetic and neurological contributions as well.

Contemporary standards for professional mental health services require basing assessments and opinions on established scientific and professional knowledge and reliable and valid information (American Psychological Association 2002). Using the forensic context as an example, in both criminal cases (e.g., competency to stand trial, the insanity defense, diminished capacity, etc.) and civil cases (e.g., child custody, adoption), the forensic professional can provide information and testimony about the mental characteristics of the designated party. Because of the inherent deception exhibited to others associated with the psychopath, one of the thorniest issues for both management/treatment and forensic purposes is detecting the possible presence of or influence from psychopathy. This limitation may hamper the forensic professional's efforts.

Since the forensic professional's role in legal proceedings is to offer specialized knowledge and expertise to the trier of fact (i.e., the judge or jury), the challenge is to have a behavioral science rationale. For this to be reliable, the forensic professional must recognize consistently and accurately when an observable or measured psychological state or trait is real versus façade.

No doubt, there has always been awareness of people deemed to suffer from or engage in conditions relevant to what is now considered to be psychopathy or sociopathy. Rather than speculate about ancient history, it is known that, from the nineteenth century on, mental health professionals have focused on so-called psychopathy. North and Yutzy (2010) mention an 1837 monograph, titled *A Treatise on Insanity and Other Disorders Affecting the Mind* (Pricard 1837), which described perverted and depraved moral principles of the mind that seem to have little or no etiology associated with prior injury and involve people who are incapable of social decency and propriety. Apparently in and around that era, there were also other references to mental conditions that might suggest awareness of psychopathy.

In the early years of psychology, the primary focus was on particular factors or ASD aspects of the human mind. In an effort to legitimize psychology, laboratory studies were emphasized. The findings eventually led to more practical considerations. Although there were undoubtedly other scholars, William James (January 11, 1842–August 26, 2010), who was often called the "Father of American Psychology," was a leader in the study of mental illness, and along with others (e.g., Adolf Meyer) promoted the teaching of psychopathology and psychotherapy in universities.

In presenting and discussing certain theoretical ideas about psychopathic characteristics, it seems appropriate to consider psychoanalytic, humanistic, and behavioral psychology.

Mental health practitioners in the late 19th century were increasingly aligned with psychoanalytic theory and were struggling with finding causation (and treatment) for cognitive, emotional, and behavior disorders. From psychoanalysis, Fenichel (1945) recognized how a person responds to guilt feelings:

> By provocation, seduction, ingratiation, and confession the environment is drawn into the conflict between the ego and the superego, in the hope of obtaining some relief. Much of what is called object relationships are actually pseudo object relationships, in which the subject does not develop any feelings toward the object as a person but uses the object as an instrument of achieving relief in a conflict with his superego (p. 166).

This use of others for one's own gratification is the cornerstone for modern viewpoints about psychopathy or ASD.

By the mid-20th century, behavioral theory did not ignore the psychopathic personality. In discussing moral principles, Wolpe (1969) said conduct in interpersonal relations included some people who "consider one's self only" and ride "roughshod over others … to get what one wants." Further, "The psychopathic personality is the extreme expression of this basic attitude, and often, of course, falls foul of society. He has not been conditioned to feel guilty or otherwise anxious in situations in which most people are so conditioned" (p. 19).

As study of the psychopathic personality developed, there was increasing awareness that certain personality characteristics supported dysfunction. From a humanistic perspective, dysfunction meant that a person was focused on being (current status) rather than becoming (committed to growth of positivism and potential). Ford and Urban (1998) said, "The result is static, undifferentiated, unfeeling, and impersonal functioning; people are unable to learn or benefit from feedback and remain stuck in their misperceptions and inadequate behavior" (p. 312).

Early on with hospitalized patients, psychopathic personality was diagnosed in 2.15% of first admissions to mental hospitals (Edwards 1957). Although it has been decades ago, Edwards held that psychopathic personality was an "Older term used to refer to a variety of … psychological personality types," (p. 653), and linked it to antisocial personality.

For "sociopathic personality disturbance," Edwards acknowledged that the patients are "often called psychopathic personalities." He further noted, "This category applies to individuals who are not classifiable as mentally defective, neurotic, or psychotic, but who manifest a marked lack of ethical or moral development and an inability to follow social approved codes of behavior" (p. 337).

Extrapolating the research and views from scholars of that period (including Karl Menninger), Edwards believed the sociopathic personality could be evidenced in:

1. Inability to understand and accept ethical values, except on a verbal level, or to pursue social acceptable goals.
2. Marked discrepancy between level of intelligence and conscience development.
3. Egocentric impulsiveness, irresponsibility, lack of restraint, and poor judgment. Prone to thrill-seeking, deviant sexual patterns, and other unconventional behavior. Callous disregard for needs and rights of others.
4. Inability to profit from mistakes and ordinary life experiences except by learning to exploit people and to escape punishment.
5. Inability to forgo immediate pleasures for future gains and long-range goals. Hedonistic, lives in the present without consideration of past or future. Unable

to withstand tedium and prone to nomad-like activities and frequent changing of jobs. External realities used for immediate personal gratification.
6. Ability to put up a good front to impress and exploit others. Often a charming, likable personality with a disarming manner and ability to win the liking and friendship of others. Often good sense of humor and generally optimistic outlook. Prone to social climbing.
7. Defective interpersonal and general social relationships. Individual usually cynical, unsympathetic, ungrateful, and remorseless in his dealings with others. Usually shows a history of difficulties with educational and/or law-enforcement authorities. No close friends.
8. Rejection of constituted authority and discipline. Individual behaves as if social regulations did not apply to him and refuses, except on a verbal level, to take any responsibility for his actions. Often shows considerable repressed hostility towards constituted authority or society in general, which may manifest itself in impulsive hostile criminal acts. Many times drifts into criminal activities but is not typically a calculating professional criminal.
9. Quick ability to rationalize and project the blame for his socially disapproved behavior. Lack of insight into his own behavior. Lies readily even though he knows he may eventually be found out by friends and acquaintances.
10. Irritating, disappointing, and distressing to others. Is frequently a great burden upon family and friends and creates a great deal of unhappiness for others. Often promises to change but rarely does so permanently—incorrigible. (p. 338)

This rather lengthy quote is given to illustrate that, even decades ago, the prevailing professional clinical views were strikingly similar to the modern-day professional clinical views, and were empirically- and evidence-based, viewpoints about the psychopathic personality. At the risk of understatement, suffice it to say, this diagnostic category has a long-standing clinical status in mental health services.

By 1968, the American Psychiatric Association's *Diagnostic and Statistical Manual of Mental Disorders-II* did not include a disorder of psychopathic disorder per se, but was seemingly included in the DSM category of personality disorders:

> This group of disorders is characterized by deeply ingrained maladaptive patterns of behavior that are perceptibly different in quality from psychotic and neurotic symptoms. Generally, these are life-long patterns, often recognizable by the time of adolescence or earlier (p. 41).

It would seem, therefore, that there is implied embrace of psychopathy.

In the foregoing edition of the DSM-II, psychopathic personality characteristics were integrated into the Category 301.7 Antisocial Personality:

> This term is reserved for individuals who are basically unsocialized and whose behavior pattern brings them repeatedly into conflict with society. They are incapable of significant loyalty to individuals, groups, or social values. They are grossly selfish, callous, irresponsible, impulsive, and unable to feel guilty or to learn from experience and punishment. Frustration tolerance is low. They tend to blame others or offer plausible rationalizations for their behavior. A mere history of repeated legal or social offenses is not sufficient to justify this diagnosis (p. 43).

The similarity of characteristics between psychopathic and antisocial conduct was evident.

With the advent of the DSM-III-R (American Psychiatric Association 1987), the Section Diagnostic Criteria 301.70 for Antisocial Personality Disorder was expanded greatly. Besides specifying a current age of at least 18, there were sections captioned "Evidence of Conduct Disorder with onset before age 15" and "A pattern of irresponsible and antisocial behavior since the age of 15," with each listing numerous behavioral indicators and with a minimum number required to qualify for the diagnosis. Similarly, the Diagnostic criteria for 301.83 Borderline Personality moved to a listing of behavioral characteristics, as did the Diagnostic criteria for 301.81 Narcissistic Personality Disorder. As will be discussed, it seems that modern views of psychopathic characteristics, contained in Antisocial Personality Disorder share similar etiologies with both borderline and narcissistic personality characteristics. The contemporary definitions of these three "pathomates" will be discussed in the next chapter.

References

American Psychiatric Association. (1968). *Diagnostic and statistical manual of mental disorders* (2nd ed.). Washington, DC: Author.

American Psychiatric Association. (1987). *Diagnostic and statistical manual of mental disorders* (3rd ed, Rev). Washington, DC: Author.

American Psychological Association. (2002). Ethical principles of psychologists and code of conduct. *American Psychologist, 57*(12), 1060–1073.

Douglas, K. S., Nikolova, N. L., Kelley, S. E., & Edens, J. F. (2015). Psychopathy. In B. L. Cutler & P. A. Zapf (Eds.), *APA handbook of forensic psychology: Individual and situational influences in criminal and civil courts* (Vol. 1, pp. 257–323). Washington, DC: American Psychological Association.

Dutton, D. G. (2003). *The abusive personality: Violence and control in intimate relationships*. New York: Guilford.

Edwards, A. L. (1957). *Techniques of attitude scale construction*. New York: Appleton-Century-Crofts.

Fenichel, O. (1945). *The psychoanalytic theory of neurosis*. New York: Norton.

Ford, D. H., & Urban, H. B. (1998). *Contemporary models of psychotherapy: A comparative analysis* (2nd ed.). New York: Wiley.

Franzoi, S. (2016). *Social psychology* (7th ed.). Redding, CA: BVT.

North, C. S., & Yutzy, S. H. (2010). *Goodwin & Guze's psychiatric diagnosis* (6th ed.). New York: Oxford University Press.

Prichard, J. C. (1835). *A treatise on insanity and other disorders affecting the mind*. London: Sherwood, Gilbert, and Piper.

Stout, M. (2005). *The sociopath next door*. New York: Broadway Books.

Wolpe, J. (1969). *The practice of behavior therapy*. Elmsford, NY: Pergamon.

Chapter 6
Definitions of Psychopathy

The previous chapter noted the links between the terms psychopathic personality and antisocial or sociopathic personality. This nexus has emerged as the modern professional viewpoint. For example, if one looks at the term "psychopathic personality" in the *APA Dictionary of Psychology,* there is no definition, only a reference to "see ANTISOCIAL PERSONALITY DISORDER" (VandenBos 2015, p. 861).

The foregoing reference source states the following three definitions that provide the substance for usage here: (1) Psychopathology—"the scientific study of mental disorders, including their theoretical underpinnings, etiology, progression, symptomatology, diagnosis, and treatment … sometimes considered synonymous with MENTAL DISORDER itself" (p. 861); (2) Psychopathy—"a synonym for ANTISOCIAL PERSONALITY DISORDER … formerly any psychological disorder or mental disease" (p. 861); and (3) Antisocial Personality Disorder—"the presence of a chronic and pervasive disposition to disregard and violate the rights of others. Manifestations include repeated violations of the law, exploitation of others, deceitfulness, impulsivity, aggressiveness, reckless disregard for the safety of self and others, and irresponsibility, accompanied by lack of guilt, remorse, and empathy" (p. 865).

Antisocial personality disorder is commonly abbreviated by the acronym ASD and is, of course, used herein, along with other (older) synonyms. ASD may also be manifested in multiple ways, such as those mentioned in the examples in the preceding paragraph. To provide a summary of ASD: "Antisocial personality (sociopathy or sociopathic personality) refers to a pattern of recurrent antisocial, delinquent, and criminal behavior that begins in childhood or early adolescence and is manifested by disturbances in many areas of life: family relations, schooling, work, military service, and marriage" (North and Yutzy 2010, p. 227). The acronym ASD is used generically, but the term psychopathy and other relative terms (as mentioned earlier) will be used knowingly to enhance the meaning of a particular statement (e.g., a quotation). It is interesting that, notwithstanding changes, none of the past terms has been totally eliminated.

R. H. Woody, *Risks of Harm from Psychopathic Individuals*, SpringerBriefs in Psychology, https://doi.org/10.1007/978-3-030-20998-8_6

Although the term ASD reveals the importance of interpersonal or social relationships, it also somewhat hampers making a definitive distinction for each of the terms. To present a possible "punch-line" at this point, perhaps the simple, yet seemingly valid, conclusion is that the psychopathic personality is void of empathy and is not necessarily criminal in nature, whereas the sociopathic personality may realize, but not care, about the hurt or harm to others and involves violations of social norms, rules, or laws (i.e., criminal conduct is common). The following elaborates on that distinction.

In human relations, empathy is a so-called "essential facilitative condition," that is, a relationship is strengthened by communications being empathic. Fox and Levin (2005) say, "lack of empathy—along with a manipulative and calculating style, an absence of remorse, and impulsiveness is frequently regarded as a defining characteristic of [both] the psychopathic and antisocial personality disorder" (pp. 63–64).

At present, a lack of empathy has not been assigned to only psychopaths but Fox and Levin point out: "Unlike psychotics, sociopaths understand the wrongfulness of their assaultive behavior. Unlike normal people, however, they understand it only at an intellectual level; the emotional component is absent" (p. 71). A sociopathic lack of affective appreciation of the effects of assaultive behavior is what negates therapeutic and rehabilitation efforts.

It is axiomatic that psychopaths may evade detection because of consciously or unconsciously feigned sociability. As noted earlier, this characteristic was captured in the title of one of the first authoritative sources on the subject, namely *The Mask of Sanity* by Cleckley (1941). He delineated ten behavioral features for psychopaths: (1) selfishness (also called egocentricity); (2) an inability to love or give genuine affection to others; (3) frequent deceitfulness or lying; (4) lack of guilt or remorsefulness (no matter how cruel the behavior); (5) callousness or a lack of empathy; (6) low anxiety proneness; (7) poor judgment and failure to learn from experience; (8) superficial charm; (9) failure to follow any life plan; and (10) cycles of unreliability. As is evident, certain of those characteristics (e.g., low anxiety and superficial charm) not only seem "normal," they can be associated with leadership! Despite the lengthy passage of time since Cleckley listed characteristics, the terms continue to have relevance.

Again being historical, the underlying motivation for psychopathic conduct may be complex and include pathologically stimulation seeking, which may have a neuropsychological basis (Quay 1965). Stated bluntly, within modern definitions, people with psychopathic features seem to be never satisfied with existing conditions, whether it is in employment, marriage, family relations, or friendships. Although their dissatisfaction is typically camouflaged (albeit that deceitful professed satisfaction may be used as a defense mechanism), psychopaths tend to be "dominant, manipulative individuals characterized by an impulsive, risk-taking and antisocial life-style who obtain their greatest thrill from diverse sexual gratification and target diverse victims over time" (Porter et al. 2000, p. 220).

Whether stimulation seeking is neurologically based or not, there is reason to believe that culture, child rearing, and life experiences may combine with social learning to produce an idiosyncratic personality structure: "Personality is an individual's unique variation on the general evolutionary design for human nature, expressed as a developing pattern of dispositional traits, characteristic adaptations, and integrative life stories complexly and differentially situated in culture" (McAdams and Pals 2006, p. 212). Consequently, it is not surprising (but it is troubling) that psychopathic features and concomitant violence can be evidenced in middle-childhood; see Bowen et al. (2002) for childhood predictors.

As said previously, the propensity for manipulation, which is present with both ASD and psychopathy in general, is manifested in disregard for and violations of the rights of others, beginning in childhood or early adolescence and continuing on into adulthood. With adults, there is apt to be: poor job performance; undependable functioning; misrepresented education and competency; early sexual experiences, perhaps promiscuous and indiscriminate (including homosexuality and prostitution); and early marriage (perhaps with infidelity, separation, and divorce). An interesting side bar, Goodwin and Guze (1989) seem to suggest that, due to parental modeling, sociopaths and psychopaths tend to marry like-minded spouses, people, stating "this is particularly true of women" (p. 244).

The bottom line in the Goodwin and Guze era was that psychopaths misrepresent and lie, often with great aplomb, acquiring and justifying their own gratification at the expense and misery of their victims (e.g., coworkers, family, and friends)—while at the same time conveying false pretenses of cordiality, competency, and caring. Sociopaths may possess some of the same sort of conduct, but extend their activities into crime or violation of societal norms.

Updating the foregoing 1989 work, North and Yutzy (2010) say that "sociopathy is common, probably increasingly so; much more frequent in males than females; more common in urban areas than rural environments and most common in low socioeconomic groups .... Individuals with sociopathy usually come from grossly disturbed families .... The prevalence of sociopathy in forensic settings and correctional settings has been estimated at 50%" (p. 230). North and Yutzy do not, however, rule out a genetic factor and note particularly, "The first manifestations may be those of the hyperactive child syndrome" (p. 230). [For a useful summary of diagnostic characteristics, see their "clinical picture" section on pp. 230–235.] They also note the importance to mental health and law-related professionals of the issue of treatment: "A major problem in treating sociopathy is the patient's lack of motivation for change .... Many therapists believe that early institutional therapy offers the only hope for success .... Psychotherapy has not achieved impressive results" (p. 238), and they do not cite any effective biological intervention.

Taking a different viewpoint on treatment and based on an extensive review of research, Douglas et al. (2015) state: "Although clinical lore has often held that highly psychopathic individuals are resistant to treatment, or even that 'treatment makes psychopaths worse,' recent research suggests more promising outcomes" (p. 257). Douglas et al. believe: "There is promise that appropriate treatment, in sufficient doses, can reduce the crime and violence of psychopathic individuals" (p. 306). Later, I will present my views, derived from my research and clinical experience, on ways to "manage" (but not "cure") ASD people in everyday life and professional human services.

A helpful source for deciding on the characteristics of psychopaths is the Psychopathic Deviate (Scale 4, with 50 items) on the Minnesota Multiphasic Personality Inventory (MMPI-2). Graham (2005b) provides the following description:

> Scale 4 was developed to identify patients diagnosed as having a psychopathic personality, asocial or amoral type. Whereas persons in the original criterion group were characterized in their everyday behavior by such delinquent acts as lying, stealing, sexual promiscuity, excessive drinking, and the like, no major criminal types were included .... The items cover a wide array of topics, including absence of satisfaction in life, family problems, delinquency, sexual problems, and difficulties with authorities .... One way of conceptualizing what Scale 4 assesses is to think of it as a measure of rebelliousness, with higher scores indicating rebellion and lower scores indicating acceptance of authority and status quo. The highest scorers on the scale rebel by acting out in antisocial and criminal ways; moderately high scorers may be rebellious but may express rebellion in more socially acceptable ways; and low scorers may be overly conventional and accepting of authority (p. 134).

Graham (2005a) indicates that high scores may be associated with difficulty incorporating the values and standards of society, and engaging in asocial, antisocial, and even criminal behaviors (e.g., lying, cheating, stealing, sexual acting out, and excessive use of alcohol and/or other drugs). There may be rebelliousness toward and conflict with authorities: "They often have stormy relationships with families, and family members tend to blame others for their difficulties. Underachievement in school, poor work history, and marital problems are also characteristic of high scorers." (p. 144)

The high scorer: is highly impulsive and adventurous; strives for immediate gratification; reveals behavior based on poor judgment and risk taking; does not benefit from experience and repeats the same mistakes; may be immature, childish, narcissistic, self-centered, selfish, egocentric, extraverted, ostentatious, socially outgoing, energetic, and exhibitionistic. Although he or she may seem likeable at first, relationships are shallow. Commonly the high scorer lacks definite and logical plans. Although he or she may feign guilt and remorse, it disappears after the crisis has passed.

In modern times, one of the most authoritative sources for the Antisocial Personality Disorder (APD) is the *Diagnostic and Statistical Manual of Mental Disorders, Fifth Edition*, commonly referred to as the *DSM-5* (American Psychiatric Association 2013). Antisocial Personality Disorder, stated in Diagnostic Criteria 301.7 include:

A. A pervasive pattern of disregard for and violation of the rights of others, occurring since age 15 and indicated by three (or more) of the following:

    1. Failure to conform to social norms with respect to lawful behaviors, as indicated by repeatedly performing acts that are grounds for arrest.
    2. Deceitfulness, as indicated by repeated lying, use of aliases, or conning others for personal profit or pleasure.
    3. Impulsivity or failure to plan ahead.
    4. Irritability and aggressiveness, as indicated by repeated physical fights or assaults.
    5. Reckless disregard for safety of self or others.

6. Consistent irresponsibility, as indicated by repeated failure to sustain consistent work behavior or honor financial obligations.
7. Lack of remorse, as indicated by being indifferent to or rationalizing having hurt, mistreated, or stolen from another.

B. The individual is at least age 18 years.
C. There is evidence of conduct disorder with onset before age 15 years.
D. The occurrence of antisocial behavior is not exclusively during the course of schizophrenia or bipolar disorders. (p. 659)

Although not determinative, the DSM-5 acknowledges a frequent lack of empathy and, "These individuals may blame the victims for being foolish, helpless, or deserving their fate" (p. 660), which seems to imply absence of empathy.

When attempting to identify the presence of APD it is important to determine "which of two or more diseases or disorders with overlapping symptoms a particular patient has" (VandenBos 2015, p. 312), also known as differential diagnosis. This is, of course, a scholarly complex and sophisticated undertaking.

Gender may be misleading: "Antisocial personality disorder is much more common in males than in females. There has been some concern that antisocial personality disorder may be underdiagnosed in females, particularly because of the emphasis on aggressive items in the definition of conduct disorder" (DSM-5, p. 662). Our society has moved to a stage in which an assured gender identity cannot be determined by a simple observation of external characteristics.

Given that psychopathy is subject to influence or reinforcement by social values, it is noteworthy that modern times may be leading "emancipated" females to engage in more criminal and violent conduct than in the past. Bartol and Bartol (2019) say that: "more recent research reports that—compared to male psychopaths—female psychopaths tend to be more subtle and skillful in their aggression, exploitative relationships, and manipulations of others, which results in their harmful acts going largely unnoticed by the authorities" (p. 274).

My research and clinical experiences support that, in accord with earlier speculation, males tend to receive a diagnosis of ASD or APD, whereas a female with many of the same characteristic would be more apt to be diagnosed as having a borderline personality disorder (*DSM-5*, Diagnostic Criteria 301.83, see p. 663).

Also, there is only limited research available on culture- and race-related issues. The *DSM-5* recommends: "In assessing antisocial traits, it is helpful for the clinician to consider the social and economic context in which the behaviors occurs" (p. 662). In a recent case in which a young African-American (A-A) man was pummeled to death by other A-A young men in a hazing incident, I was told by a mature and intelligent A-A man that, "there should not be prosecution, hitting a person in a hazing ritual is common in the Black community" (which may or may not be true or generalizable).

This chapter has provided a review of terminologies relevant to psychopathy, along with specific characteristics. I pointed out that, although the terms changed over time, the characteristics remained much the same. As said early on, I consider the term psychopath to include the wide range of terms discussed here, and if one of the other terms is used, the substance of the term presented will be clarified. The *Mask of Sanity* statement by Cleckley (1941) seems to capture the general scope of psychopathy, notwithstanding the term that is being discussed.

References

American Psychiatric Association. (2013). *Diagnostic and statistical manual of mental disorders* (5th ed.). Washington, DC: Author.

Bartol, C. R., & Bartol, A. M. (2019). *Introduction to forensic psychology* (5th ed.). Thousand Oaks, CA: Sage.

Bowen, G. L., Bowen, N. K., Richman, J. M., & Woolley, M. E. (2002). Reducing school violence: A social capacity framework. In L. A. Rapp-Paglicci, A. R. Roberts, & J. S. Wodarski (Eds.), *Handbook of violence* (pp. 305–325). New York: John Wiley.

Cleckley, H. (1941). *The mask of sanity*. St. Louis, MO: C. V. Mosby.

Douglas, K. S., Nikolova, N. L., Kelley, S. E., & Edens, J. F. (2015). Psychopathy. In B. L. Cutler & P. A. Zapf (Eds.), *APA handbook of forensic psychology: Individual and situational influences in criminal and civil courts* (Vol. 1, pp. 257–323). Washington, DC: American Psychological Association.

Fox, J. A., & Levin, J. (2005). *Extreme killing: Understanding serial and mass murder*. Thousand Oaks, CA: Sage.

Goodwin, D. W., & Guze, S. B. (1989). *Psychiatric diagnosis* (4th ed.). New York: Oxford University Press.

Graham, J. R. (2005a). Characteristics of high and low scores on the MMPI-2 clinical scales. In G. P. Koocher, J. C. Norcross, & S. S. Hill III (Eds.), *Psychologists' desk reference* (2nd ed., pp. 141–149). New York: Oxford University Press.

Graham, J. R. (2005b). Clinical scales of the MMPI-2. In G. P. Koocher, J. C. Norcross, & S. S. Hill III (Eds.), *Psychologists' desk reference* (2nd ed., pp. 132–136). New York: Oxford University Press.

McAdams, D. P., & Pals, J. L. (2006). A new big five: Fundamental principles for an integrative science of personality. *American Psychologist, 61*(3), 204–217.

North, C. S., & Yutzy, S. H. (2010). *Goodwin & Guze's psychiatric diagnosis* (6th ed.). New York: Oxford University Press.

Porter, S., Fairweather, D., Drugge, J., Hervé, H., Birt, A., & Boer, D. P. (2000). Profiles of psychopathy in incarcerated sexual offenders. *Criminal Justice and Behavior, 27,* 216–233.

Quay, H. C. (1965). Psychopathic personality as pathological stimulation-seeking. *American Journal of Psychiatry, 122*(2), 180–183. https://doi.org/10.1176/ajp.122.2.180.

VandenBos, G. R. (2015). *APA dictionary of psychology* (2nd ed.). Washington, DC: American Psychological Association.

Chapter 7
Incidence of Psychopathy

When considering the epidemiological data relevant to psychopathy, there are four major problems:

First, the definition of psychopathy has not been consistent, resulting in "apples and oranges" estimates of incidence (i.e., an estimate may or may not include both ASD and psychopathy and may fail to provide the distinction).
Second, cultural factors influence the definition that exists at any one point in time. For example, historical documents reveal that in the early American Psychiatric Association 2013s, physicians were in controversy over "moral insanity," such as whether the "morally insane" should/could be committed to mental hospitals or declared insane by the courts (Goodwin and Guze 1989). Since "culture" changes, literally and figuratively, "with the times," the definition of a psychopath has been subject to countless changing conditions or factors, such as serial divorces and marriages (e.g., someone who has had multiple divorces and remarried several times), sexual preferences and orientation, financial strategies, and so on.
Third, data collection has usually been on a particular (rather than diverse) sample, such as prisoners, outpatients in a psychiatric facility, schools, etc.
Fourth, the appearance of propriety, competency, and sociability allows many psychopaths to go undetected and to not be included in estimates of incidence.
With these four points in mind, the incidence (how widespread) and prevalence (the proportion of cases in the population) presented below should be considered not as adequate, but as meriting awareness. They are somewhat ambiguous, but may shed some light on what may be the incidence. More detailed epidemiological studies, dealing with numerous methodological issues, are greatly needed.

With the foregoing caveat, Hare (1996, 1999) has provided noteworthy research on psychopathy. His research seems to support that psychopathy is: present in about one in 100 people in the United States; higher in the United States than in certain other countries; and on the increase in the United States (if not elsewhere as well). More will be said later about the cultural factors that may be associated with these conditions.

R. H. Woody, *Risks of Harm from Psychopathic Individuals*, SpringerBriefs in Psychology, https://doi.org/10.1007/978-3-030-20998-8_7

Since researchers still vacillate between and often interchange the two terms psychopath and sociopath, confidence in incidence and prevalence is unjustified. Looking at the research on mental disorders in the general population, Karpiak and Norcross (2005) note that there is a 3.5% prevalence of overall antisocial personality disorders, an average of 5.8% for males and 1.2% for females. Since these figures are derived from clinical diagnostic records and those not seeking treatment would not be included, this may be an underestimate. Goodwin and Guze (1989) offer a different estimate, saying, "15 percent of male and 3% of female psychiatric outpatients were sociopaths" (p. 243). Again, it seems that ASD and psychopathy are lumped together, and those without clinical contacts would not be included.

Reaching for the overall population (i.e., including those who are not criminal violators or have not sought mental health services), Stout (2005) opines:

> About one in twenty-five individuals is sociopathic, meaning, essentially, that they do not have a conscience. It is not that this group fails to grasp the difference between good and bad; it is that the distinction fails to limit their behavior .... Without the slightest blip of guilt or remorse, one in twenty-five people can do anything at all (p. 9).

Stout acknowledges that sociopaths are not necessarily violent per se, but she points out how costly the dissonance or turmoil caused by the high incidence of sociopathy is for society, with damage to relationships, bank accounts, self-esteem, and peace of mind.

For Antisocial Personality Disorders (Diagnostic Criteria 301.7), the *DSM-5* (2013) indicates the following:

> Twelve-month prevalence rates of antisocial personality disorder, using criteria from previous *DSMs*, are between 0.02% and 2.2%. The highest prevalence of antisocial personality disorder (greater than 70%) is among most severe samples of males with alcohol use disorder and from substance abuse clinics, prisons, or other forensic settings. Prevalence is high in samples affected by adverse socioeconomic (i.e., poverty) or sociocultural (i.e., migration) factors (p. 661).

Given my special concern about borderline personality disorders, the *DSM-5* states:

> The median population prevalence of borderline personality disorder is estimated to be 1.6% but may be as high as 5.9%. The prevalence of borderline personality disorder is about 6% in primary care settings, about 10% among individuals seen in outpatient mental health clinics, and about 20% among psychiatric inpatients. The prevalence of borderline personality disorder may decrease in older age groups (p. 665).

Despite the evidence-basis for the two foregoing *DSM-5* quotations, it is prudent to caution that there are countless factors that could create, diminish, exacerbate, or mask prevalence issues for ASD, APD, and borderline personality disorder.

Let us discuss certain factors. Assume that two research studies (both with respectable methodology, analysis, and interpretation) produce different incidence and prevalence. Since no universal or definitive causation can be assumed justly, it is necessary to recognize that a personality can spring from, say, a genetic or neurological condition, but still be influenced to varying degrees by social reinforcement. The nature of APD and ASD puts the values of society in the spotlight.

It is indisputable that modern society, certainly in Western countries, is far more complex, for good or bad, than in bygone eras. The concomitant is a plethora of social reinforcements impinging on everyone. Hays (2016) indicates that modern cultural influences include: age and generation; developmental or other disability; religion and spiritual orientation; ethnic and racial identity; socioeconomic status; sexual orientation; indigenous heritage; national origin; and gender. Hays issues a caution against diagnosing personality disorders, due to perceptions from the social field: "the specific criteria constituting a personality disorder will vary depending on the interpersonal skills and attitudes valued by a culture at any given point in time" (p. 207).

Now back to the topic of prevalence. If the imposition of a diagnosis of personality disorder is the product of social reinforcement (to some unknown degree), it seems logical that societal conditions will impact the diagnosis. With regret, it seems that conditions in modern society (e.g., especially from the mass media, violent video games, ways to avoid personal responsibilities, and diminished social values) promulgate more reinforcement of antisocial behavior than at times in the past.

Consequently, this viewpoint suggests that the incidence and prevalence of APD and ASD are more apt to increase than decrease (consider the epidemic of incarcerations in the correctional system, and the concomitant of drug-related and violent crimes now versus in previous decades). Acknowledging that I have no crystal ball, I believe that essentially all prevalence reports relevant to personality disorders, including APD, ASD, and borderline personality disorder, are on an upward trajectory.

References

American Psychiatric Association. (2013). *Diagnostic and statistical manual of mental disorders* (5th ed.). Washington, DC: Author.

Goodwin, D. W., & Guze, S. B. (1989). *Psychiatric diagnosis* (4th ed.). New York: Oxford University Press.

Hare, R. D. (1996). Psychopathy: A clinical construct whose time has come. *Criminal Justice and Behavior, 23,* 25–54.

Hare, R. D. (1999). *Without conscience: The disturbing world of the psychopaths among us*. New York: Guilford.

Hays, P. A. (2016). *Addressing cultural complexities in practice* (3rd ed.). Washington, DC: American Psychological Association.

Karpiak, C. P., & Norcross, J. C. (2005). Lifetime prevalence of mental disorders in the general population. In G. P. Koocher, J. C. Norcross, & S. S. Hill III (Eds.), *Psychologists' desk reference* (2nd ed., pp. 3–7). New York: Oxford University Press.

Stout, M. (2005). *The sociopath next door.* New York: Broadway Books.

Chapter 8
Violence and Criminal Psychopathy

Since psychopaths are unrelentingly dedicated to self-gratification, any barrier that they encounter may potentially trigger subversive or retaliatory aggression, which can easily escalate to violence. Hare (1996) states: "The ease with which psychopaths engage in … dispassionate violence has a very real significance for society in general and for law enforcement personnel in particular" (p. 58). He notes that about half of law enforcement officers who die in the line of duty are killed by psychopaths.

To be clear, all persons characterized by psychopathy do not resort to violence per se. Some may, for example, channel their aggression into legal or even constructive activities. That said, the self-serving nature of psychopathy seems to construct a potential for the aggressive propensity to be manifested in hostility.

To summarize the linkage between psychopathy and violence, the motivation derived from psychopathy creates, under certain circumstances, a propensity for violence. There is an important distinction: although some nonpsychopaths reveal affect when they are violent, criminal psychopaths are callous and cold blooded when they act violently. Criminal psychopaths often become violent in domestic scenarios for revenge or retribution, and disinhibition can be exacerbated by alcohol and other drugs.

Since sexuality is such a strong determinant of conduct, psychopathic aggression and violence often occur in stressful or ego-threatening situations. Hart and Dempster (1997) indicate that rapists with psychopathic characteristics tend to do crimes for nonsexual motivations, such as anger, vindictiveness, sadism, and opportunism. Hare (1996) cites research that shows that, in federal prisons, psychopaths make up 26.1% of rapists, 18.3% of mixed sex offenders (including child molesters), and 5.4% of incest offenders, which supports that a reasonable estimate seems to be that about one-third (or more) of sexual offenders are psychopaths.

Although incarceration is society's current placement of choice for criminals, there is no just reason to believe that imprisonment alone cures or modifies the criminal conduct of psychopaths. Psychopaths violate parole more than nonpsychopaths (33% vs. 7%), and within eight years of release from prison, 80% of psychopaths are rearrested (Quinsey et al. 1995). Indeed, among sex offenders who receive treatment,

R. H. Woody, *Risks of Harm from Psychopathic Individuals*, SpringerBriefs in Psychology, https://doi.org/10.1007/978-3-030-20998-8_8

Hare (1996) indicates that the psychopaths are the most likely to recidivate early and often (e.g., 80% vs. 20%)! Note that the psychopathic recidivists do not, however, necessarily commit sexual violations per se.

Gretton et al. (2001) indicate that criminal psychopaths, much like psychopaths in general, "lack a normal sense of ethics and morality, live by their own rules, are prone to use cold-blooded, instrumental intimidation and violence to satisfy their wants and needs, and generally are contemptuous of social norms and the rights of others" (p. 428). Relying on manifested violence and aggression, criminal psychopaths engage in abuse, threats, and intimidation much more than other types of people. More will be said later about violence.

Among mental health professionals, there seems to be near-unanimous endorsement of the research on psychopathy conducted by Robert D. Hare, professor emeritus at the University of British Columbia. His research is the basis for his book, *Without Conscience: The Disturbing World of the Psychopaths Among Us* (Hare 1999). In considering psychopathy, Hare states the emotional/interpersonal characteristics include: glib and superficial, egocentric and grandiose, lack of remorse or guilt, lack of empathy, deceitful and manipulative, and shallow emotions; and the social deviance characteristics are: impulsive, poor behavior controls, need for excitement, lack of responsibility, early behavior problems, and adult antisocial behavior.

Regarding the term sociopath, it appears that about 50–80% of the U.S. prison population qualifies for being a sociopath, and about 11–25% of prison inmates qualify for the term psychopath—yet these inmates commit about 50% of the total number of violent crimes (Hare 1998). Among the incarcerated, 15.5% of women prisoners are psychopaths and 25–30% of male prisoners are psychopaths; and as compared to male psychopaths, female psychopaths seem to be less aggressive and less violent, but there is contradictory evidence as to whether females recidivate less often (Bartol and Bartol 2015).

Among female offenders, Salekin et al. (1997) identified two types of psychopaths: One group lacked empathy or guilt, had engaged in interpersonal deception, and were sensation seeking and prone to boredom. The other group had early behavioral problems, promiscuous sexual behavior, and nonviolent adult antisocial acts. Consideration of the reports pertaining to female offenders raises the question of whether an increase in female violence has a link to an increase in psychopathy or to an increase in antisocial (criminal) behavior?

On the issue of race, Bartol and Bartol (2019) seem to support that there are minimal, if any, differences between African-American (A-A) and Caucasian psychopaths, although A-A criminal psychopaths tend to be less impulsive than White criminal psychopaths. They appear to believe there is no difference in incidence between incarcerated A-A and Caucasian females.

Finally, society is becoming fed up with psychopathy and sociopathy: "it seems to be generally believed that psychopaths are difficult to treat because (a) they are an extreme, qualitative distinct category; (b) psychopathy is extremely persistent throughout life; (c) psychopathy has biological causes which cannot be changed by psychosocial interventions; and (d) the lying, conning, and manipulativeness of psychopaths make them treatment resistant" (Farrington 2005, pp. 494–495).

Consequently, there may be greater negativity about psychopaths in the criminal justice system (e.g., sentencing), which may result in high incarceration rates and longer sentences.

The legal system appears to be more and more negative about defendants with psychopathic characteristics. Skeem et al. (2003) report: "There is evidence that psychopathy increasingly is being used as an aggravating factor in the sentencing phase of US death penalty cases, where it has been argued that the presence of these personality traits renders a defendant a 'continuing threat to society'" (p. 17). If this assertion is true, one could wonder: if there continues to be no effective treatment and society chooses to continue to favor incarceration and increases the use of psychopathy as an aggravating factor, is it just a matter of time until society will extend severity in sentencing to include the death penalty for crimes other than murder—such as repeated drug dealers and pedophiles?

References

Bartol, C. R., & Bartol, A. M. (2015). *Introduction to forensic psychology* (4th ed.). Thousand Oaks, CA: Sage.

Bartol, C. R., & Bartol, A. M. (2019). *Introduction to forensic psychology* (5th ed.). Los Angeles: Sage.

Farrington, D. C. (2005). The importance of child and adolescent psychopathy. *Journal of Abnormal Child Psychology, 33,* 489–497.

Gretton, H. M., McBride, M., Hare, R. D., O'Shaughnessy, R., & Kumka, G. (2001). Psychopathy and recidivism in adolescent sex offenders. *Criminal Justice and Behavior, 28,* 427–449.

Hare, R. D. (1996). Psychopathy: A clinical construct whose time has come. *Criminal Justice and Behavior, 23,* 25–54.

Hare, R. D. (1998). Psychopathy affect, and behavior. In D. Cooke, A. Forth, & R. Hare (Eds.), *Psychopathy: Theory, research, and implications for society*. Dordrecht, The Netherlands: Kluwer.

Hare, R. D. (1999). *Without conscience: The disturbing world of the psychopaths among us*. New York: Guilford.

Hart, S. D., & Dempster, R. J. (1997). Impulsivity and psychopathy. In C. D. Webster & M. A. Jackson (Eds.), *Impulsivity: Theory, assessment, and treatment*. New York: Guilford.

Quinsey, V. L., Rice, M. E., & Harris, G. T. (1995). Actuarial prediction of sexual recidivism. *Journal of Interpersonal Violence, 10,* 85–105.

Salekin, R. T., Rogers, R., & Sewell, K. W. (1997). Construct validity of psychopathy in a female offender sample: A multitrait-multimethod evaluation. *Journal of Abnormal Psychology, 106,* 576–585.

Skeem, J. L., Edens, J. F., & Colwell, L. H. (2003, April). Are there racial differences in levels of psychopathy? A meta-analysis. Paper presented at the 3rd annual conference of the International Association of Forensic Mental Health Services, Miami, FL.

Chapter 9
Relationships with Psychopaths

As will be recalled, earlier chapters tracked through the evolution of human characteristics that eventuated in establishing, maintaining, and refining the definition of psychopathy. In sum, there have been many definitions or sets of characteristics. An authoritative source, such as *Diagnostic and Statistical Manual* (*DSM*) series from the American Psychiatric Association, have provided numerous criteria for psychopathic characteristics.

This chapter deals with recognizing a psychopath who is on the cusp of entering or has entered into one's life. As mentioned previously, one of the earliest twentieth century widely accepted diagnoses was posited by Cleckley (1941). As stated earlier in this book, he believed that the behavioral characteristics of a psychopath may include factors that are not readily evident. To purposefully repeat, Cleckley delineated ten behavioral features for psychopaths: selfishness (also called egocentricity); (2) an inability to love or give genuine affection to others; (3) frequent deceitfulness or lying; (4) lack of guilt or remorsefulness (no matter how cruel the behavior); (5) callousness or a lack of empathy; (6) low anxiety proneness; (7) poor judgment and failure to learn from experience; (8) superficial charm; (9) failure to follow any life plan; (10) cycles of unreliability.

It should be mentioned that, from time to time, the number of Cleckley behavioral characteristics has varied from, say, twenty-one to sixteen to the ten above. This wide range led DeLisi (2016) to say critically: "Cleckley was consistently inconsistent in his view of the role of antisocial conduct as diagnostic of psychopathology" (p. 29). Although there have been, through the years, many modifications and adaptations, even the most current authorities seem to adhere, at least in general, to Cleckley's fundamental notions.

As a side excursion, a few biographical comments about two of the foremost researches relevant to psychopathology, Hervey M. Cleckley, MD, and Robert D. Hare, Ph.D., merit consideration. Their works seem to move from clinical observation to statistical (factor) analysis.

R. H. Woody, *Risks of Harm from Psychopathic Individuals*, SpringerBriefs in Psychology, https://doi.org/10.1007/978-3-030-20998-8_9

Hervey M. Cleckley was an American psychiatrist, working extensively in a locked mental hospital. He believed that the patient with a psychopathic personality mimicked a normally functioning person, while harboring a chaotic internal personality structure that would lead to purposeful destructive behavior that could harm the psychopath as well as other people. He thought that everyone could, at times, reveal illogical behaviors and beliefs. These views, derived largely from clinical or subjective analysis, led to the more objective contemporary views of Robert D. Hare.

Many researchers in the behavioral and health care professions consider Canadian Robert D. Hare to be the foremost contemporary source of impressive research on psychopaths. Although beyond the scope of critique per se, his development of checklists for identifying characteristics of psychopathy is superior.

Hare and colleagues have been prolific for research on how persons with psychopathic status are to be found in all areas of life, such as in the context of employment, politics, leadership, and professionalism. He makes it clear that a psychopath can excel in many ways, yet be influenced by psychopathy. As would be expected of a behavioral scientist, Hare's research has led to various modifications in his empirically based views about psychopathic behavior.

At this point, one or a few characteristics that seem to be associated with psychopathy should not be used to "diagnose" the condition. When considering key symptoms of psychopathy, Hare (1999) cautions against using the symptoms to diagnose self or others; he believes that a diagnosis requires explicit training, and an expert opinion and "services should be obtained from a qualified (registered) forensic psychologist or psychiatrist" (p. 34).

It is Hare's view that psychopathy involves a cluster or syndrome of symptoms that are inter-related. He alleges that a psychopathic person is prone to be a "chronically unstable and aimless lifestyle marked by casual and flagrant violations of social norms and expectations" (p. 57).

9.1 Recognizing Behavioral Features of Psychopaths

To detect a possible psychopath, there should be consideration of possible feelings, the nature of the relationships, and social deviance. There are two classes of key symptoms. The first category, emotional/interpersonal includes: glib and superficial, egocentric and grandiose, lack of remorse or guilt, lack of empathy, deceitful and manipulative, and shallow emotions. The second category, social deviance, includes: impulsive, poor behavior controls, need for excitement, lack of responsibility, early behavior problems, and adult antisocial behavior.

As stated in the preceding paragraphs, the status of "psychopath" should not be imposed simply because of the presence (chronic or occasional) of some of the symptoms. This caution is applicable to the ten core behavioral features identified by Hare (1999):

1. Poor judgment and failure to learn from experience
2. Trouble evaluating the potential consequences of their actions
3. Lack of guilt or remorsefulness for cruel and antisocial actions
4. Callousness and lack of empathy
5. Low anxiety or nervousness in high-pressure situations
6. Cycles of unreliability and impulsiveness
7. Superficial Charm
8. Frequent deceitfulness or lying
9. Failure to follow a well-defined life plan
10. Inability to love or give genuine affection to others.

Hare's underlying assumption was that a psychopath might not have all or a certain number of these ten features, but the ones that they did possess would be stable.

From 1993 (the original copyright date of Hare's basic treatise), there has been a plethora of behavioral science research investigations that have sought to identify critical factors. Throughout the array of research, there has been a commitment to advancing measurement and assessment of possible cues to the existence of psychopathy.

In the ensuing years, there have been seemingly countless empirically based clusters of factors, with the robust groupings resulting in Hare's *Psychopathy Checklist—Revised* (*PCL-R*), which has been applied to literally tens of thousands of evaluations each year (Otto and Heilbrun 2002). The *Checklist* has continued to attract extensive research and, consequently, revisions. Bartol and Bartol (2015) say, "the instrument provides researchers and mental health professionals with a universal measurement for the assessment of psychopathy that facilitates international and cross-cultural communication concerning theory research, and eventual clinical practice" (p. 23).

After extensive research, including with statistical factor analysis, the work of Hare and his countless colleagues supports four factors that constitute psychopathy: Affective (Arrogant and Deceitful Interpersonal Style); Deficient Affective Experience; Impulsive Lifestyle and Behavioral (unstable and irresponsible Behavioral Style); and Antisocial Behavior (Douglas et al. 2015; see p. 264).

The preceding assessment-oriented information provides clues for inferring and recognizing the possible presence of psychopathic symptoms. This is an essential prerequisite for predicting the presence of psychopathy, which might otherwise go undetected because of the so-called "mask of sanity."

The lifestyle characteristics of the psychopath tend to be antisocial: "Lack of realistic life goals is an unreasonable, unfeasible sense of one's life achievements relative to the investment one makes" (DeLisi 2016, p. 34). There is impulsivity and parasitic orientation, or as DeLisi states:

> a desire to exploit or live off the material support of another person .... The emotional deficits that psychopathic individuals present generally reduce their capacity to have true, deep engagement with others. Narcissism or grandiose self-worth is an extreme love for oneself. Narcissism is doubly important in that it contributes to the blind pursuit of selfish needs at the expense of others. Pathological lying is the repeated use of lying and deception to explain, defend, and justify one's conduct (p. 34).

Needless to say, antisocial inclinations can certainly create dissonance in all sorts of relationships, be it with marriage, co-workers, or service recipients. Narcissism fuels adversity. In everyday life, it seems that the constructs possessed by a psychopathic individual may well be harmful to social propriety or positive relationships in virtually any context, but they need not be criminal per se.

In legal decisions, nowadays there are generally negative views about a defendant with psychopathic features. Indeed, with some differences being present between jurisdictions, evidence of psychopathy, perhaps based (in part) on the *PCL-R*, may constitute prove to be a negative mental condition for a defense against an alleged crime or deciding on a sentence.

9.2 Psychopaths in Everyday Life

Given the scholarly substance of research on psychopathy, especially from Hare and DeLisi, and the numerous other related definitions that have been set forth in the preceding chapters, the subsequent discussion will selectively rely on: lack of empathy, poor emotional controls, dishonesty, and narcissism. As described via the information provided in the preceding chapters, there could be other categories. However, along with a possibility of antisocial or criminal conduct surfacing later on, these four categories seemingly provide a reasonable frame for recognizing, dealing with, and avoiding interpersonal relations with a psychopathic family member or friend.

Lack of empathy or empathic failure means that the person has “a lack of understanding of another person’s feelings, perceptions, and thoughts” (VandenBos 2015, p. 365). In healthy family relations and friendships, there should be reciprocal and accurate empathic communications. Whether with a child or adult in the family or social circle, impaired empathy may result in confusion, hurt feelings, or sense of non-caring.

Poor emotional controls is relevant to feeling vulnerable and problems with emotional adjustment, such as inappropriate anger or withdrawal for affective relations. The person lacks effective management of “the condition or process of personal acceptance of and adaptation of one’s circumstances which may require modification of attitudes and the expression of emotions that are appropriate to a given situation” (p. 363). There may be an inability to maintain emotional cognition that could be essential for recognizing interpreting the emotions of others. That is, the person may believe incorrectly that the positive cues are absent.

Consciously or unconsciously, dishonesty leads the person to not tell the truth. There may be attempts at deception, which refers to “any distortion of or withholding of fact with the purpose of misleading others” (p. 286). Dishonesty and lying are close akin to distortion: “either the unconscious process of altering emotions and thoughts that are unacceptable in the individual’s psyche or the conscious misrepresentation of facts, which often serve the same underlying purpose of disguising that which is unacceptable to or in the self” (p. 326).

Dealing with psychopathic characteristics requires as much objectivity as the human conditions allow. When there is a familial or social relationship, regardless of degree of positivism or negativity, the persons are prone to apply subjectivity, that is, pass the perceived characteristic though a filter of subjectivity. Positive bias must be lessened. For affective communications, there should be efforts to concretize underlying meanings, which will help truthfulness and accuracy of comprehension.

There is an effort to prove the adjectival percepts.

Any bias may or may not be acknowledged or controlled. When emotions are involved, as seems to be inevitable with potentially all human relations, there may be attributions to the other person that distort or influence the bases for interpersonal communications. Consequently, when one of the persons in any sort of relationship, such as with a family member or friend, communicates or behaves in a manner that denigrates or harms another person, the possibility of psychopathy has been elevated.

As with any negative encounter, a possibility of psychopathy justifies avoidance. However, it is illogical to allege that the solution will always be to "walk away." There are some relationships that do not accommodate distancing as a solution (e.g., co-workers, marriage, family, and the list goes on). Nonetheless, there should be a staunch dedication to not tolerating emotional or physical abuse, and any plausible, viable, and lawful remedies should be considered and actions taken to reverse or eliminate the abusive manifestation.

References

Babiak, P., & Hare, R. D. (2006). *Snakes in suits: When psychopaths go to work*. New York: Harper/Collins.

Bartol, C. R., & Bartol, A. M. (2015). *Introduction to forensic psychology* (4th ed.). Thousand Oaks, CA: Sage.

Bloom, B. (Ed.). (1956). *Taxonomy of educational objectives: The classification of educational goals*. New York: Longman, Green.

Cleckley, H. (1941). *The mask of sanity*. St. Louis, MO: C. V. Mosby.

DeLisi, M. (2016). *Psychopathology as unified theory of crime*. New York: Palgrave Macmillan.

Douglas, K. S., Nikolova, N. L., Kelley, S. E., & Edens, J. F. (2015). Psychopathy. In B. L. Cutler & P. A. Zapf (Eds.), *APA handbook of forensic psychology: Individual and situational influences in criminal and civil courts* (Vol. 1, pp. 257–323). Washington, DC: American Psychological Association.

Dutton, D. G. (2003). *The abusive personality: Violence and control in intimate relationships*. New York: Guilford.

Gacono, C. B., Nieberding, R. J., Owen, A., Rubel, J., & Bodholdt, R. (1997). Treating conduct disorder, antisocial, and psychopathic personalities. In J. B. Ashford, B. D. Sales, & W. H. Reid (Eds.), *Treating adult and juvenile offenders with special needs* (pp. 99–129). Washington, DC: American Psychological Association.

Hare, R. D. (1999). *Without conscience: The disturbing world of the psychopaths among us*. New York: Guilford.

Heilbrun, A. B. (1982). Cognitive models of criminal violence based upon intelligence and psychopathy levels. *Journal of Consulting and Clinical Psychology, 50*, 546–557.

Lipsey, M., & Wilson, D. B. (1993). The efficacy of psychological, educational and behavioral treatment. *American Psychologist, 48*(120), 1181–1209.

MacKenzie, J. (2015). *Psychopath free*. New York: Berkley (Penguin, Random House).
McIvor, R. J., & Petch, E. (2006). Stalking of mental health professionals. *British Journal of Psychiatry, 188,* 403–404.
Otto, R., & Heibrun, K. (2002). The practice of forensic psychology: A look toward the future in light of the past. *American Psychologist, 57*(1), 5–18.
VandenBos, G. R. (2015). *APA dictionary of psychology* (2nd ed.). Washington, DC: American Psychological Association.
Woody, R. H. (1988). *Fifty ways to avoid malpractice*. Sarasota, FL: Professional Resource Exchange.
Woody, R. H. (1997). *Legally safe mental health practice.* Madison, CT: International Universities Press (Psychosocial Press).
Woody, R. H. (2000). Professional ethics, regulatory licensing, and malpractice complaints. In F. W. Kaslow (Ed.), *Handbook of couple and family forensics* (pp. 461–474). New York: John Wiley.
Woody, R. H. (2004). *Group therapy: An integrative cognitive social-learning approach*. Sarasota, FL: Professional Resource Press.

Chapter 10
The Victim's Personal Rights

Although a bit strange perhaps, it seems that a goodly number of people find it difficult advocate and exercise effective self-protection. This is certainly evident when a potentially harmful person is a family member or presumed friend. When psychopathy is present, kinship or friendship should not prevent actions to stop harm to oneself or others.

A cornerstone for protection of self and others is tethered to respect for life. As described previously, a person with psychopathic characteristics may act in way that will harm others, perhaps even violating the law or the moral principles of society, friends, or family.

Obviously the laws adopted by a society do not sanction assaults on others—unless it is in service to a greater good (e.g., to stop abuse of one's self or another person). The preceding comment is exemplified by the common law principle (and in some jurisdictions, by statutory law) that a person can "step into the shoes" of a potential victim to prevent the infliction of harm to that person from an attacker, psychopathic or otherwise.

Regrettably, because of the trauma of lifelong abuse, some victims lack self-respect and tolerate abuse and violence. Once I came upon a scene in which a male had a female on the ground and was punching her forcefully. As I dashed towards them to "rescue" her from the violence, she looked up and shouted, "Don't hurt him, he's my boyfriend!"

At this point, it is important to acknowledge that modern law protects the rights of everyone, regardless of age, race, nationality, or whatever. Likewise, no personal characteristic justifies imposing unjust harm to or usurping the legal rights of anyone else. Most certainly, there are laws that contradict criminal conduct, as could be applicable to the way in which a family member or friend mistreats someone.

Said differently, in a democracy, effective government controls and defines human behavior. As described throughout this book, there are legal processes that assure equal protection for all citizens, unless justified by laws to the contrary. The hallowed Constitution of the United States supports, among other rights and privileges, due process for all alleged violators of laws. However, the same person is not free to

R. H. Woody, *Risks of Harm from Psychopathic Individuals*, SpringerBriefs in Psychology, https://doi.org/10.1007/978-3-030-20998-8_10

harm others unjustly, which means, of course, that some psychopathic acts can be prosecuted.

From an early age, every person should seek to understand the United States Constitution, which is applicable at all levels of society. Among other things, it establishes the nature, function, and limits of government (e.g., balancing the power between the legislative, executive, and judicial branches). Referred to as the Bill of Rights, the first ten amendments include individual liberties, such as the freedom of religion, speech, and the press, as well as the right to "keep and bear arms," the right to privacy and security (e.g., no illegal search and seizure), and other restrictions on the government. A critical social psychological principle is that the Constitution establishes equal protection and due process, as the basis for legal action in all jurisdictions, whether it is national, state, or local.

The two principles do mean that when an offense is alleged, a law enforcement officer (LEO) or the everyday person cannot violate the rights of an alleged offender. This restriction introduces an important principle for dealing properly with possible harm from, say, a psychopathic person. The punch line should be obvious: When a person senses the possible occurrence of abuse, neglect, or assault, the corrective action should not be self-help—he or she should leave the scene and/or contact law enforcement. There should absolutely be no tolerance of usurping one's rights or allowing harm to occur.

Of great importance, adhering to the recommendation of eliminating psychopathic conduct from one's life space (e.g., exiting the presence of the potentially harmful person) and seeking protective actions from a bona fide law enforcement source is of significance importance to overall function of social order. Although some folks might hesitate to accept the foregoing declaration (i.e., leaving or law enforcement) a bit difficult to accept (especially if a family member or friend is the subject of the action), to feed the pathology by accepting the harm is, in itself, a form of pathology. Of course, if harm is unavoidable, self defense (or defense of others) is potentially appropriate (as an instructor of defensive tactics often said, "all bets are off" and "you do what you have to do").

10.1 Benefiting Society

Leaving and/or bringing law enforcement into one's life to avoid abuse from a psychopathic individual actually benefits the psychopathic family member or friend, but there is even a greater good. The foregoing action model creates several options to guide the would-be offender into a helpful relationship, such as with a qualified mental health professional (e.g., psychologist, psychiatrist, mental health counselor, marriage and family therapist, clinical social worker, and so on).

Regrettably, it is commonly difficult to change the chronic and deep-seated nature of a character disorder, and a psychopathic personality structure is certainly no exception. Indeed, many professionals believe that a psychopathic disorder is commonly thought to be virtually impossible to remediate or to "cure" it (i.e., restructure it to being, say, nonviolent, non-manipulative, or honest in interactions with others). At best, a realistic goal, again assuming the victim has not exited or law enforcement has not intervened, would be to manage the pathology (i.e., no tolerance of manifestations of character dysfunctions).

The preceding framework offers a positive course of action. It should be apparent that possible victims, as well as the psychopathic person, benefit from reinforcement of constructive characters (e.g., being truthful), and not condoning the negative factors (e.g., lying) that were set forth and elaborated on in the earlier chapters. Moreover, improving a society will occur by lessening or ameliorating adverse behavior, even if it is accomplished one person at a time.

10.2 Criminalizing Psychopathy

Since psychopathy is known to resist change, such as accepting responsibility for one's anti-social behaviors, it is tempting to advocate isolation of the psychopath, such as via criminal prosecution. The classic movie "Clockwork Orange," directed by Stanley Kubrick (1971), based on a 1962 novel by Anthony Burgess, depicted the use of profound intervention by brain surgery to remove the neurological triggers to pathology and violence. Similarly, there have been (and still are) advocates of chemical or surgical castration to eliminate repeat offensives and procreation of psychopaths, and incarceration to isolate the psychopaths.

Law enforcement is dedicated to public safety and the Constitutional rights of everyone in the particular society. Any action allowed in a democratic society should be on behalf of the welfare and safety of law-abiding members of the society, and promote the society as a whole.

Criminal prosecution of psychopaths may allegedly, purposefully, or inadvertently cross into contradiction of the tenets of democracy. Any action accepted by a democratic society must strengthen the society, safeguard the rights of the people therein, and remedy a proven violation of criminal law.

In a democratic society, the foremost objective allows laws to be a means for social control to accomplish and maintain an ordered society. Logically, any punishment should be rooted in harm-prevention theory. It should be in service to rehabilitation. Thus, the question "can psychopaths be rehabilitated" defies, to date, an authoritative answer (i.e., some interventions, including residential programs, have produced positive results, while others have not). Simply said, as per the Eighth Amendment of the Constitution, punishment cannot be cruel and unusual, as would shock the conscience of a civilized society.

10.3 Morality

The term morality is best defined as the beliefs and values that society considers as appropriate standards for acceptable and proper behavior in a given context. For example, historically society pervasively banned public nudity. Rightly or wrongly, there are some areas, including (for example) private "resorts," cruises, and even public beaches (e.g., in California and Florida) that are potentially exempt from laws that would lead to prosecution for nudity (with certain limitations). In other words, over time the values of society on this matter have changed. The same potential change can be aligned with essentially any conduct related to morality.

Further, the definition of morality is influenced and shaped by the particular context (e.g., being at home, a public place, a health care facility) and the persons who are "actors" in the situation (e.g., family members, work-related colleagues, and so on). In other words, to some extent the context for the conduct and relationship between the persons determines the moral tenets that they should accept or reject.

As might be assumed from the preceding comments, defining morality is highly subjective. Rather than reflecting any personal views (and since this is a book on psychology), consideration should be again given to definitions from the American Psychological Association (VandenBos 2015). Therein, the word "morality" is defined as "a system of beliefs or set of values relating to right conduct, against which behavior is judged to be acceptable or unacceptable" (p. 667), and "moral relativism" is "the belief that the morality or immorality of an action is determined by social custom rather than by universality or fixed standard of right and wrong" (p. 668).

In the foregoing definition, the term context refers to the conditions or circumstance in which a particular act occurs. The term morality is in a contextual and temporal framework, a definition by time and place (and conditions therein), that is, the beliefs and values that society considers as appropriate standards for proper behavior in a given context. With few and limited exceptions because of cultural values (e.g., religious), contemporary western civilization is hard and fast in opposing harm being inflicted on, for example, family or friends—or anyone else, except under warlike conditions.

To summarize, societal values and laws do not accommodate inflicting harm on another person. Even if the harmful action was unintentional, such as in an accident (which by definition is commonly not considered to be intended), the person who caused the negative action or outcome is potentially held accountable. That is, the person causing the harm must "pay the price" which could be financial (e.g., the cost to repair or make the injured person whole, albeit that, regrettably, sometimes an injury or death may never be voided or the victimized person "made whole").

The victim of harm from psychopathic conduct has a legal and moral right to exact a remedy from the miscreant. It is to the victim's credit to avoid any additional or future harm or injury, whether it by appropriate self-help or legal actions. Victims should be mindful that modern society does not encourage imprudent self-help; strong preference is allotted to reliance of law enforcement. To not adopt possible safeguards can be, however, a discredit to the victim (e.g., contributory negligence). Said bluntly, encounters with a person with psychopathic characteristics should be avoided if possible and legal actions should be immediate to thwart any further harm.

10.4 Communicating with a Psychopathic Person

As a threshold for the topic of communicating with a psychopath, two characteristics should be acknowledged. First, all communications should pass through a psychopathic filter. Second, anything expressed by the psychopath may be later denied, altered, rescinded, or prove to be untruthful. For example, a psychopathic person's promise that "I will change my behavior" may not have a grain of truth—this is, of course, the reason that any form of therapy has no surefire credibility with a psychopath spouse or friend.

Some mental health professionals may be prone to rely on and promote seemingly empathic qualities in the interventions provided to a psychopath. Criticism has been stated that such an empathy-promoting approach may actually teach a means for further psychopathic deception; that is, the psychopathic person may learn how to appear to be other than what is truthful. This might accommodate camouflaged pathology, such as an erudite or highly intelligent psychopath's gaining entry a person's (i.e., potential victim's) life.

Of course there could be situations for which contextual factors contradict the victim's exiting or isolating a psychopathic, say, family member (e.g., "for the good of the children"). Although understandable, there may come a time when relying on law enforcement or taking legal action (e.g., dissolution of the relationship, obtaining a restrain order, criminal prosecution) may be the only healthy and lawful action.

References

VandenBos, G. R. (2015). *APA dictionary of psychology* (2nd ed.). Washington, DC: American Psychological Association.

Stanley, K. (1971). A clockwork orange. Hawk Films.

Chapter 11
Managing the Great Pretender

As mentioned earlier, there are different views among law enforcement and mental health professionals about treatment for psychopathy. In part, the negativity comes from doubtful treatment efficacy. One continuing view is that there is "nothing the behavioral sciences can offer for treating those with psychopathy" (Gacono et al. 1997, p. 119). As Dutton (2003) puts it: "There is some question, of course, of whether or not psychopaths are treatable at all," but he acknowledges that the research of being "untreatable is far from conclusive" (p. 181).

The core of the problem may be that psychopaths feign positive qualities and profess to remedy any deficits that are challenged. In support of the negative view, stated bluntly, both noncriminal and criminal psychopaths will mask or avoid acknowledging their problem behavior, and they lack insight into the nature and extent of their disturbance. Consequently, they have no sincere motivation to change. Rather they resort to refining and seeking opportunities for their devious conduct in order to retain their self-gratifying psychopathy.

When dealing with psychopaths, the professional who aims to promote the positive effects of empathy may see the person transform this quality into tactics for hurtful purposes. Finding high levels of empathy among intelligent psychopaths, Heilbrun (1982) suggested that psychopaths develop "enormous powers of empathic discernment—albeit for the purposes of self-aggrandizement" (p. 557). In other words, since violent acts, like inflicting pain and suffering, are intentional, "empathic skills promote the arousal and satisfaction of sadistic objectives by enhancing the criminal's awareness of the pain being experienced by his victim" (Fox and Levin 2005, p. 64).

As a means for grading the fallibility of psychological opinions, consider the following three questions: Could therapeutic interventions intended to create empathy actually provide the psychopath with additional techniques for deceitful behavior? Could a person in litigation falsely portray attitudes and values or act out behaviors that could lead another person (even an astute judicial legalist or a mental health professional) to see that portrayal as empathy? Could not alleged serial killers and serial sexual offenders have adopted pathologically motivated empathy as a psychological

R. H. Woody, *Risks of Harm from Psychopathic Individuals*, SpringerBriefs in Psychology, https://doi.org/10.1007/978-3-030-20998-8_11

characteristic (which could be used, perhaps, to lure victims or gain leniency from the criminal justice system)?

The term "manage" refers to applying knowledge to decision making about using resources in a particular context. "Bloom's taxonomy" holds that managed experiences should progress through knowledge, comprehension, application, analysis, synthesis, and evaluation (Bloom 1956). When applied to managing a Great Pretender, there should be strong cognitive processes in play (e.g., plans based on logical substance). There must be recognition of reality, including the fact that some Great Pretenders openly or covertly defy management.

A cornerstone for a management plan for dealing with Great Pretenders is survival. The person must be committed to self-protection (as well as protecting certain others, such as minor offspring). Hare (1999) offers general guidelines: (1) identify and know with what you are dealing (e.g., rely on evidence-based knowledge; (2) guard against ingratiation, manipulations, and seductive appeals, etc. (i.e., one of the primary tools of psychopathy); (3) take a broad view (i.e., keep your eyes wide open for subtle cues); (4) stay "on guard" for protection against a "sneak attack"; and (5) cultivate self-understanding and high self-esteem.

In addition, the research from Hare supports relying on healthy support sources (e.g., friends and family proven to be trustworthy), avoiding power struggles, and maintaining firm rules for every relationship. Worries and concerns about specific abusive behaviors should be shared with trusted persons, as this sharing may be critical in a potential criminal charge. Regardless of circumstances, permanent and substantial change of deception and manipulation should not be expected. There may (likely?) come a time when the contacts with a Great Pretender will need to be terminated FULLY. There can be no safe and healthy relationship with someone plagued by psychopathy.

As mentioned, self-protection and protection of loved ones should always be foremost in one's values. This includes protecting all persons (and possibly pets) in the household who are caught up in the pathological web of risk and abuse, be it via neglect or physical or emotional abuse.

I have said repeatedly, "trust no one." Although philosophically, such a suggestion might seem overly negative, especially since modern society allows some conditions that will inevitably accommodate Great Pretenders' potentially entering into anyone's life.

I believe that the person targeted by a Great Pretender to be a victim should adopt a pledge to assert recognition of possible psychopathic behavior. I suggest that this protective stance can be accomplished by: (1) never tolerating unjustified criticism; (2) carefully scrutinizing every primary relationship for harmful encounters; (3) considering whether treatment by another person is sincere and well intended (i.e., honorable, evaluated as objectively as possible); (4) never accepting any lying, condescension, patronizing, sarcasm, or dismissive accusations (e.g., jealousy); (5) requiring every ongoing relationship to be mutual and equal, with no disproportionate control and power; (6) terminating (i.e., walking away from) contacts with anyone with seeming psychopathic characteristics; (7) making no impulsive decisions; and (6) seeking qualified support and help when needed (MacKenzie 2015).

Said bluntly, even a scintilla of evidence of threat, falsity, or violence should be the basis for immediately terminating contacts with and avoiding the particular person in the future, albeit often there may be a "price" to pay for the decision. Of great importance, physical or emotional abuse should always be reported to law enforcement. Understandably, this viewpoint is too often considered to be particularly challenging for an intimate partner in a presumably committed relationship with a person with psychopathic behaviors.

As a reminder, a psychopath's promises of "I'll change" or "I will never do it again" are not to be believed. If a relationship with a psychopath is terminated, the closure should be considered final. There should be no going back. In the event that the parties decide that the relationship can potentially be restored, an apology is inadequate. There must be monitoring and recording of indelible and irrefutable proof of a constructive change. When sociopathic or psychopathic behaviors are present, more often than not, optimism is foolish and self defense against allowing invasive reunions must forever be maintained.

11.1 Conclusion

Earlier in this book, three psychological theories were mentioned: psychoanalytic, humanistic, and behavior. In professional mental health or human services interventions, those three theoretical approaches can be integrated. Here is my framework for a professional theoretical melding. [Note: although a layperson may not be able to adopt these treatment principles per se, the ideas should be useful for self-guidance.]

From my clinical experience and research, I believe that psychoanalytic ideas are highly useful for explaining possible unconscious or unintended motivations, humanistic conditions can set standards for and possibly strengthen the interpersonal communications, and behavioral strategies can bring about cognitive and conduct changes. Dutton (2003) states: "of all treatment modalities, structured, cognitive-behavioral treatments based on social learning theories have better effects on antisocial behavior than other modes of treatment" (p. 182).

As one who is committed strongly to an integrative cognitive social-learning approach for group interventions (Woody 2004), it is interesting that a meta-analysis of group services for psychopaths found positive results (Lipsey and Wilson 1993). To be effective (i.e., bring about constructive conduct, the social-emotional involvement of a treatment or intervention group must be structured to reinforce positive ideas and behavior.

Despite my support of group interventions, I have grave concern about bringing psychopaths together and believe that such togetherness carries special risk of manipulations and volatility that could contradict a worthy intervention. To be effective, there must be astute group leadership by a well-trained professional; that is, self-help groups are risky.

From the total body of research on psychopathy and my own research and experiences, my viewpoint is: when encountering a person with psychopathic personality characteristics, regardless of context or other circumstances, potential victims should always maintain a strong self-defense, and implement it consistently and in many different forms. In other words, to avoid being victimized, recall the old saw, "Keep your wagons in a circle!"

Harboring a notion that a person with psychopathic personality characteristics can be changed readily is naïve at best. Change may occur, but it will not be assuredly accomplished. Relying on the research on psychopaths by Hare (1998), Dutton (2003) offers several warnings: (1) Efficacy for psychotherapy is doubtful because of transference and other emotional types of relationships are unlikely. (2) There is pathological lying, negating honest communication with a mental health professional (or anyone). (3) There is a lack of motivation due to grandiosity and lack of guilt. (4) In therapeutic interventions or helpful efforts there will be superficial role playing. (5) Rejection of responsibility for actions is common. (6) Therapeutic and helpful modalities do not provide adequate motivating stimulation. He summarizes: "Psychopaths lack the ability to develop emotional relationships with significant others and with therapists, do not see themselves as having a psychological problem, and according to some studies, are the worst recidivists" (p. 181).

Again referring to the valued research on psychopaths by Hare, scholarly or evidence-based information has yielded knowledge of psychopathy, which is essential for mental health professionals' own self-protection and the human services interventions that they design. Hopefully, the information has provided fundamental learning on critical issues. A concomitant for both laypersons and professional helpers is to have self-understanding, which provides much needed strength for endurance, wisdom, and efficacy in dealing with ASD characteristics.

Mental health professionals should be aware that imposing a diagnostic label, such as psychopathic personality, even if seemingly justified, could do more harm than good. Said differently, diagnostic labels may harden the psychopathic characteristics. At the same time, the professional should rely on strict diagnostic criteria and not resort to some innocuous (lesser) substitute category. Certainly adherence to the *DSM-V* criteria is appropriate. When doing a diagnosis and deciding on an intervention, there is a definite need for caution.

Allies, such as family members or friends, can be either extremely supportive or contradictory to change efforts. Anyone involved in efforts to manage psychopathic behavior should have safeguards against his or her personal feelings (e.g., self-doubts, shame, anger, wish for vindication, etc.) creating impediments to positive outcomes.

Although written for professional health human services, the guidelines for dealing with a psychopath that are provided by Babiak and Hare (2006) construct a structure that can be useful in almost any sort of relationship involving possible psychopathy. A critical principle to remember is that if a situation does not work out to the satisfaction of the psychopath, the would-be helper will be blamed. Consequently, Babiak and Hare advise the following: (1) There should be strong boundaries; keep singular and limited roles. (2) Maintain well-defined and firm control, do not let a psychopath manipulate or be commanding. (3) Do not take anything said by a psychopath as being assuredly true or accurate; and confirm information and alleged facts. (4) Be cautious about any reported potentially negative past or present conduct, such as criminal record, substance abuse, violence, etc. (5) Discount flattery and ingratiating comments, which are warning signs of a likelihood of future warfare attempted with and denunciation of the would-be helper. (6) For legal purposes, keep a private written record (e.g., a document that possibly justifies an intervention by law enforcement later on); place a copy with a trusted other.

In service to self-protection, even a mental health professional should "trust no one." Some professional training programs seek to indoctrinate students with the notion that "unconditional positive regard" is mandatory for effective helping. That idea is useful, perhaps even "essential" in professional relationships, but should be maintained only to a point. If a psychopathic person tries to impose or create negative conditions, expectations, or intrusions, mental health and human services professionals should appropriately and tactfully terminate services. Self-sacrifice by a professional will only exacerbate the negative effects of psychopathy.

Above all else, whether a law enforcement or mental health professional or a layperson dealing with a friend, co-worker/employee, acquaintance, spouse/partner, or family member with psychopathic characteristics, priority should be given to maintaining personal safety, dignity, and rights, and avoiding confrontations. Trying to confront someone with psychopathy will likely be viewed as an affront and challenging, and abusive or violent conduct might ensue. Said bluntly, if there is no clear-cut interpersonal structure that assures psychological and physical well being, stopping contact with a psychopathic person is most often the best solution, which may require involvement by law enforcement.

If there is an increase in psychopathy, it may be due to influence from cultural changes that evolve over the years (e.g., permissiveness). Certain societal conditions seem to provide a fertile breeding ground for narcissism and irresponsibility.

Negative influences from the mass media (e.g., violence on television) deserve substantial professional attention. The demise of the community mental health system has definitely resulted in many people today being left with an unfulfilled need for psychological services. Reliance on outpatient private practitioners of mental health or human services, especially with the restrictions imposed by government regulations and managed care, all too often lead to inappropriate or inadequate use of professional services; for example, there are psychopaths who need inpatient placements, but are left to sporadic outpatient "band-aid" approaches. In turn, difficult and threatening clients and increasingly victimizing practitioners (Woody 1988, 1997, 2000; McIvor and Petch 2006).

Despite denials and protestations, the Great Pretender is commonly part of injurious relationships, with a potential for violent acts. Many (most?) psychopaths, disguised by a "mask of sanity," violate the rights of others (including crimes, albeit without being detected by law enforcement agencies or subjected to the criminal justice system). [I was appalled when a social worker was beaten during a home visit to a psychopath, and the judge denied her a judgment, saying: "that sort of thing is part of the job.]

References

Babiak, P., & Hare, R. D. (2006). *Snakes in suits: When psychopaths go to work*. New York: Harper/Collins.
Bloom, B. (Ed.). (1956). Taxonomy of educational objectives: The classification of educational goals. New York: Longman, Green.
Dutton, D. G. (2003). *The abusive personality: Violence and control in intimate relationships*. New York: Guilford.
Fox, J. A., & Levin, J. (2005). *Extreme killing: Understanding serial and mass murder*. Thousand Oaks, CA: Sage.
Gacono, C. B., Nieberding, R. J., Owen, A., Rubel, J., & Bodholdt, R. (1997). Treating conduct disorder, antisocial, and psychopathic personalities. In J. B. Ashford, B. D. Sales, & W. H. Reid (Eds.), *Treating adult and juvenile offenders with special needs* (pp. 99–129). Washington, DC: American Psychological Association.
Hare, R. D. (1998). Psychopathy affect, and behavior. In D. Cooke, A. Forth, & R. Hare (Eds.), *Psychopathy: Theory, research, and implications for society*. Dordrecht, The Netherlands: Kluwer.
Hare, R. D. (1999). *Without conscience: The disturbing world of the psychopaths among us*. New York: Guilford.
Heilbrun, A. B. (1982). Cognitive models of criminal violence based upon intelligence and psychopathy levels. *Journal of Consulting and Clinical Psychology, 50*, 546–557.
Lipsey, M., & Wilson, D. B. (1993). The efficacy of psychological, educational and behavioral treatment. *American Psychologist, 48*(120, 1181–1209.
MacKenzie, J. (2015). *Psychopath free*. New York: Berkley (Penguin, Random House).
McIvor, R. J., & Petch, E. (2006). Stalking of mental health professionals. *British Journal of Psychiatry, 188*, 403–404.
Woody, R. H. (1988). *Fifty ways to avoid malpractice*. Sarasota, FL: Professional Resource Exchange.
Woody, R. H. (1997). *Legally safe mental health practice*. Madison, CT: International Universities Press (Psychosocial Press).
Woody, R. H. (2000). Professional ethics, regulatory licensing, and malpractice complaints. In F. W. Kaslow (Ed.), *Handbook of couple and family forensics* (pp. 461–474). New York: John Wiley.
Woody, R. H. (2004). *Group therapy: An integrative cognitive social-learning approach*. Sarasota, FL: Professional Resource Press.

Index

R. H. Woody, *Risks of Harm from Psychopathic Individuals*, SpringerBriefs in Psychology, https://doi.org/10.1007/978-3-030-20998-8

MIX
Papier aus verantwortungsvollen Quellen
Paper from responsible sources
FSC® C105338

FSC
www.fsc.org

If you have any concerns about our products,
you can contact us on
ProductSafety@springernature.com

In case Publisher is established outside the EU,
the EU authorized representative is:
Springer Nature Customer Service Center GmbH
Europaplatz 3, 69115 Heidelberg, Germany

Printed by Libri Plureos GmbH
in Hamburg, Germany